Essential Math Series

The Essential Guide to Competition Math
Number Theory

유하림(Harim Yoo) 지음

The Essential Guide to **Competition Math**
[Number Theory]

초판 발행 2022년 3월 11일

저자 유하림
발행처 헤르몬하우스
발행인 최영민

주소 경기도 파주시 신촌로 16
전화 031-8071-0088
팩스 031-942-8688
전자우편 hermonh@naver.com
출판등록 2015년 03월 27일
등록번호 제406-2015-31호
인쇄제작 미래피앤피

ISBN 979-11-91188-69-1 53410

Copyright ⓒ 2022 by Harim Yoo
First edition Printed 2022. Printed in Korea.

• 헤르몬하우스는 피앤피북의 임프린트입니다.
• 이 책의 어느 부분도 저작권자나 발행인의 승인 없이 무단 복제하여 이용할 수 없습니다.
• 파본 및 낙장은 구입하신 서점에서 교환하여 드립니다.
• 정가는 뒤표지에 있습니다.

Preface

To. 학부모님과 학생들께

경시수학 입문용 교재로 집필한 The Essential Guide to Competition Math(Fundamentals)이 출간된 이후, 여러 가지 생각을 했습니다. 현재 다양한 수학경시대회에서 출제되고 있는 문제들의 난이도는 흔히 얘기하는 킬러 문형들이 많은데, 입문용 교재에 들어가 있는 문제의 난이도는 초중급 난이도가 더 많아서, 이 둘 사이의 간격을 좁힐수 있는 방법이 무엇일까 고민하게 되었습니다. 이 고민에 대해 제가 내린 결론은 준킬러 문형들을 많이 공부할 수 있는 교재가 필요하다는 것이었습니다. 현재 경시대회를 준비하려고 하는 학생들과 수업하면서, 계속해서 가다듬고 피드백 받고, 연구원을 통하여, 계속 문제 난이도 조절을 하다가 이번 기회에 출간을 하게 되었습니다.

입문용 교재로 공부가 끝난 학생들에게 킬러 문형을 풀기 직전 연습을 해야 하는 문제들 위주로 작성을 했고, 여러 피드백을 받아보니, 준킬러 문형에 해당하는 문제들을 훨씬 많이 포함하고 있어서 상위권 학생들에게는 복습의 기회가 되고, 상위권으로 올라가야 할 학생들에게는 필요한 든든한 디딤돌 같은 역할을 하기에 적합하다는 평이 많았습니다.

이전 교재와 마찬가지로 교재 제목인 Essential Guide가 암시하듯, 핵심 문제들로 구성되어 있어, 150쪽 내외의 교재이지만, 책을 구성하고 있는 문제들은 모두 하나하나 경시수학을 준비하려는 학생들에게 필요한 문제들입니다. 입문용 교재를 volume 1이라고 생각한다면, 이 교재는 volume 2, 그리고 추후에 나올 교재들은 모두 volume 3, 4 등과 같은 방식으로 유기적으로 관계를 맺고 있는 교재들로 작업하고 있으니, 입문용 교재를 공부한 후, 이 교재로 학습하면 크게 도움이 될 것으로 생각합니다.

이 교재를 출간할 수 있도록 물심양면으로 힘써주신 마스터프렙 권주근 대표님께 감사합니다. 또한, 저에게 항상 롤모델이 되어주고, 강사로서 성장할 수 있는 원동력을 주시고 계신 심현성 대표님께 진심으로 감사의 마음을 전합니다. 현재 저의 여러 교재 검수를 맡고 있는 든든한 안준규 제자에게도 감사의 마음을 전합니다. 언제나 든든한 지원군인 제 아내와 딸, 부모님께도 항상 감사합니다. 마지막으로, 제 삶에 이러한 기회를 주신 하나님께 감사드리며, 앞으로도 더 좋은 교재를 만들어 견고하고 튼튼한 유하림 커리큘럼을 완성하도록 하겠습니다.

2021년 겨울
유하림

이 책의 특징

유하림 커리큘럼 Essential Math Series 경시 시험 대비를 위한 책 중 AMC 10(12), CEMC, ARML Local, Purple Comet Math Meet, Spirit of Math and Stanford SMILE International Contest와 같은 시험을 대비하는 교재입니다. AMC 10을 이미 시작하는 8, 9, 10학년 한국 학생들이 AIME Qualification을 받기 위해 공부해야 하는 필독서가 되길 바라는 마음으로 집필하였습니다. 현재 미국 명문 Boarding School 및 국내외 외국인 학교에 다니는 8, 9, 10학년 학생들이 AMC 10(12) 및 다른 경시 시험에서 실제로 적극적으로 사고(think)하고, 문제 풀이의 방향을 잡을 수 있길 바라면서 책을 썼습니다.

실력을 기르기에 최적화된 교재

경시수학 관련하여 압구정 현장 강의에서 많은 학생들을 교육하였고, 실제로 이런 문제들을 포함한 수업을 듣다가, 경시수학에 연을 맺어, MIT 및 Stanford와 같이 유수의 학교로 간 제자들이 많습니다. 위 제자들을 가르치며, 핵심 개념과 복잡한 문제풀이의 그 중간과정에서 가장 많이 고민했던 유형들의 문제들과 다양한 개념의 융합된 형태의 문제들을 적절히 섞어두었습니다. 특히, 준킬러 문형들이 많이 포함되어 있기 때문에, 해설지를 상세히 공부해가며, 여러 가지 측면으로 푸는 연습을 하길 바랍니다. 위 책은 현장 강의에서 가장 좋은 피드백을 받은 문제들 위주로 작성한 교재이므로, AMC 10/12의 Number Theory 문제들을 공략하기 위해 작성된 교재입니다.

✌️ 생각의 확장을 위한 교재

Number Theory를 배울 때, 쉽게 생각하는 부분부터 해서 현재 문제 출제 방향에 가장 적합하게 서술했으며, 실제 경시대회 문형들의 최고난이도 문제보다는 쉽게, 다만 그 문제를 풀기 위해 반드시 알아야 하는 방향을 제시하는 교재로 집필하였습니다. 문제 유형으로 나누어 설명하는 것보다, Number Theory의 주제들에 적용되는 다양한 사고 방식을 서술하였으며, 이들이 어떻게 합쳐지면서 문제 풀이에 적용되는지 체감하며 공부할 수 있는 교재입니다.

🤟 유학 준비생을 위한 바로 그 교재

교과 수학보다 응용의 폭이 깊어서, 시작조차 엄두를 내지 못했던 유학생들과 그 준비생들에게 하나의 지름길이 될 수 있기를 희망하면서 집필한 책입니다. 노스웨스턴 대학교 학창시절 수학에 대한 열정을 뒤늦게 꽃피워 밤새워 공부했고, 저는 학생들을 더 잘 가르치고, 더 나은 미래로 이끌기 위해, AMC, AIME, Stanford SMILE, ARML, HMMT, PUMaC, SUMO와 같은 문제들을 동일한 열정으로 끊임없이 풀고 해석합니다. 여러분이 지금 보는 이 책은 제 현재 노력의 최선의 산실이며, 앞으로도 그러할 것입니다. 이 책을 통해 수학을 두려워하지 않고, 문제 해결을 즐거워하며, 이른 나이에 수학에 대한 열정을 꽃피우길 기대합니다.

CONTENTS

Preface 3
이 책의 특징 4

TOPIC 1 Divisor and Remainders 9
   1.1 Divisor and Remainders 10
   1.2 Parity and More 13
   1.3 Prime Factorization 23
        Practice 27

TOPIC 2 Least Common Multiple and Greatest Common Divisor 35
   2.1 Least Common Multiple 36
        Practice 39
   2.2 Greatest Common Divisor 46
        Practice 49
   2.3 Eulidean Algorithm and Bezout's Identity 56
        Practice 60
   2.4 Application of LCM and GCD 68
        Practice 71

TOPIC 3 Counting Divisors and More Arithmetic   79

    3.1   Counting Divisors and More Arithmetic 80

            Practice 83

TOPIC 4 Base-N Expression   97

    4.1   Base-N Expression 98

            Practice 101

TOPIC 5 Modular Arithmetic   115

    5.1   Basic Knowledge of Modular Arithmetic 116

            Practice 119

    5.2   Application of Modular Arithmetic 126

            Practice 130

TOPIC 6 Mixed Practice   139

TOPIC 1

Divisor and Remainders

1.1 Divisor and Remainders

Let n be a natural number. If it is divided by d, then there uniquely exists some integers q and r such that $n = d \cdot q + r$ where $0 \leq r < d$. For instance, if 12 is divided by 5, then the quotient must be 2 with the remainder of 2. In short, $12 = 5 \cdot 2 + 2$. It is crucial to make sure that the remainder non-negative, less than the divisor. We can easily extend n to $\mathbb{Z}$, the set of integers. One important idea to remember is that the remainder must be in the interval $[0, |d|)$.

Example Divide -13 by 5 to find out the unique quotient and remainder.

Step-by-Step Solution
\# 1. Notice that -13 is NOT divisible by 5. There must be a remainder from the list $\{0, 1, 2, 3, 4\}$.
\# 2. Let $r = 1$. Then, $-13 = 5q + 1$ implies that $-14 = 5q$, which has no solution.
\# 3. Let $r = 2$. Then, $-13 = 5q + 2$ implies that $-15 = 5q$, so $q = -3$.
\# 4. Since q and r are unique, we conclude that $-13 = 5(-3) + 2$. In particular, if $n = dq + r < 0$, we may find m and q_{min} such that $m > 0$, $q_{min} > 0$ and $n + mq_{min} > 0$, i.e., $-13 + 3 \cdot 5 = -13 + 15 = 2 > 0$.

If $r = 0$, then we say d is a divisor of n. It means that there exists some integer q such that $n = dq$. In this case, $|d| \leq |n|$, and $|d|$ divides $|n|$ (which seems bit obvious). This helps us a lot when we divide algebraic expression by another expression.

Example If $n^2 + n + 1$ divides 3, where n is an integer, find all values of n.

Step-by-Step Solution
\# 1. $|n^2 + n + 1| \leq 3$, so $|n^2 + n + 1| = 0, 1, 2, 3$.
\# 2. Since $n^2 + n + 1$ is a divisor of 3, we solve for $n^2 + n + 1 = \pm 1, \pm 3$.
\# 3. $n^2 + n + 1 = 1$ implies that $n = 0, -1$. Similarly, $n^2 + n + 1 = -1$ implies that there exists no integer value of n satisfying the given equation.
\# 4. $n^2 + n + 1 = 3$ implies that $n = -2, 1$. Similarly, $n^2 + n + 1 = -3$ implies that there exists no integer value of n satisfying the given equation.

Example If $n^2 + n + 1$ divides $2n + 3$, where n is a natural number, find all values of n.

Step-by-Step Solution
\# 1. $|n^2 + n + 1| \leq |2n + 3|$, so $n^2 + n + 1 \leq 2n + 3$.
\# 2. $n^2 - n - 2 \leq 0$ implies $(n + 1)(n - 2) \leq 0$.
\# 3. $n = -1, 0, 1, 2$, but n must be natural, so $n \neq -1, 0$.
\# 4. If $n = 1$, then, $n^2 + n + 1 = 3$ but $2n + 3 = 5$, so 3 does not divide 5.
\# 5. If $n = 2$, then $n^2 + n + 1 = 7$, and $2n + 3 = 7$, so 7 divides 7.
\# 6. The only possible value of n is 2.

Basic Drill 1

1. Divide 2021 by 43 to determine its remainder.

2. If $n + 2$ divides 10, find out all possible values of n that are natural numbers.

3. If $n > 7$ is divided by 7, find out all possible remainders.

4. If $n + 2$ is a factor of $4n + 2$, find out all possible integer values of n.

Answer to Basic Drill 1

1.

$$2021 = 43 \cdot 47 + 0$$

implying that 2021 is divisible by 43 with the quotient of 47. This illustrates that 43 is a divisor of 2021. Hence, the remainder is $\boxed{0}$.

2.
Since $n \geq 1$, we notice that $n + 2 \geq 3$. On the other hand, the positive divisors of 10 can be listed as $\{1, 2, 5, 10\}$. Since divisors of 10 greater than 3 are either 5 or 10, we solve $n + 2 = 5, 10$ for n. Hence, $\boxed{n = 3, 8}$.

3.
Using division algorithm, write $n = 7q + r$ where q is a quotient and r is the remainder. Since $|r| < 7$, we can write all possible values of r as $\boxed{\{0, 1, 2, 3, 4, 5, 6\}}$.

4.

$$\frac{4n+2}{n+2} = \frac{4(n+2) - 6}{n+2}$$
$$= 4 - \frac{6}{n+2}$$

implying that $n + 2$ must be a divisor of 6. Since n is an integer, $n + 2 = \pm 1, \pm 2, \pm 3, \pm 6$. Hence, $\boxed{n = -3, -1, -4, 0, 1, -5, -8, 4}$.

1.2 Parity and More

Though this theme is NOT strictly "mathematical," it is helpful for us to know why we care about "remainders." The fundamental idea of looking at remainders is to group "infinitely" many items into "finite" bundles. The most renowned, commonly-used idea of grouping is the well-known **parity**.

- Even integer : $\{\cdots, -2, 0, 2, \cdots\}$ where each element n can be written as $n = 2k$ for some integer k.

- Odd integer : $\{\cdots, -3, -1, 1, 3, \cdots\}$ where each element n can be written as $n = 2k + 1$ for some integer k.

The idea of even/oddness is used most of the times in competition math, especially when we see number theory problems. However, this does not have to be limited to "parity."

For instance, if the set of integers is divided into three bundles, it must be best for us to see the remainder when an integer is divided by 3. In other words, we may categorize the set of integers into $Z_0 = \{\cdots, -3, 0, 3, 6, \cdots\}$, $Z_1 = \{\cdots, -2, 1, 4, 7, \cdots\}$, and $Z_2 = \{\cdots, -1, 2, 5, 8, \cdots\}$.

Another way of writing down the categorization of the set of natural numbers with distinct remainder is to use the following set-up.

- $n = 3k + 0$, or $n \equiv 0 \pmod{3}$.

- $n = 3k + 1$, or $n \equiv 1 \pmod{3}$.

- $n = 3k + 2$, or $n \equiv 2 \pmod{3}$.

As seen above, $n \equiv r \pmod{p}$ implies that $n = pk + r$ for some integer k. This is known as "modular arithmetic," which will be covered in detail in later topics and detailed solution of practice questions. That being said, let us go over some examples of modular arithmetic to see how they work.

Example $n \equiv 2 \pmod{5}$ implies $n = 5k + 2$ for some integer k, so $n = \{\cdots, -3, 2, 7, \cdots\}$.

Example $6n \equiv -2 \pmod{5}$ implies $1n \equiv 3 \pmod{5}$ since $6 \equiv 1 \pmod{5}$ and $-2 \equiv 3 \pmod{5}$. In particular, $6n - \mathbf{5n} \equiv -2 + \mathbf{5} \pmod{5}$.

Example $25 \cdot 13 \equiv 1 \cdot 1 \pmod{12}$, since $25 \equiv 1 \pmod{12}$ and $13 \equiv 1 \pmod{12}$. In particular, $25 = 12 \cdot 2 + 1$ and $13 = 12 \cdot 1 + 1$.

Basic Drill 2

1. Solve $3n \equiv 6 \pmod{8}$ for n.

2. Solve for $4n \equiv 8 \pmod{12}$ for n.

3. Solve for all integer pairs (x, y) satisfying $x^2 - y^2 = 5$.

4. Solve for all whole number pairs (x, y) satisfying $x^2 - y^2 = 16$.

Answer to Basic Drill 2

1.

$$3n \equiv 6 \pmod{8}$$
$$\overset{1}{\cancel{3}} n \equiv \overset{2}{\cancel{6}} \pmod{8}$$
$$n \equiv 2 \pmod{8}$$

implying that $n = 8k + 2$ for some integer k. Hence, $\boxed{n \in \{\cdots, -6, 2, 10, 18, \cdots\}}$.

2.

$$4n \equiv 8 \pmod{12}$$
$$\overset{1}{\cancel{4}} n \equiv \overset{2}{\cancel{8}} \pmod{\cancel{12}^3}$$
$$n \equiv 2 \pmod{3}$$

implying that $n = 3k + 2$ for some integer k. Hence, $\boxed{n \in \{\cdots, -1, 2, 5, 8, \cdots\}}$. As one can see from question 1 and 2, if residue modulo n has a common factor, we must cancel it out altogether.

3.

$$x^2 - y^2 = (x-y)(x+y)$$
$$(x-y)(x+y) = \text{even} \cdot \text{even or odd} \cdot \text{odd}$$
$$(x-y)(x+y) = 1 \cdot 5$$
$$= -1 \cdot -5$$
$$= 5 \cdot 1$$
$$= -5 \cdot -1$$

implying that $\boxed{(x,y) = (3,2), (-3,-2), (3,-2), (-3,2)}$.

4.

$$x^2 - y^2 = (x-y)(x+y)$$
$$(x-y)(x+y) = 2 \cdot 8$$
$$= 4 \cdot 4$$

implying that $\boxed{(x,y) = (5,3), (4,0)}$. One should easily see why we looked at $2 \cdot 8$ and $4 \cdot 4$, because $x - y$ and $x + y$ have equal parities, and $x - y \leq x + y$.

Practice

1. How many different counting numbers (or natural numbers) will each leave a remainder of 5 when divided into 54?
(A) 1
(B) 2
(C) 3
(D) 4
(E) 5

2. Every 5 months, John must replace his phone to a newer one. He changed it the first time in May. In what month will it be changed the 27th time?
(A) January
(B) February
(C) March
(D) April
(E) May

3. April is "month equivalent" to its square number of months. In particular, $4^2 \equiv 4$ (mod 12). Which of the following could be "month equivalent" to its square number of months?
(A) June
(B) July
(C) August
(D) September
(E) October

4. A lilypad with 200 pads is numbered from 1 to 200. Dylan the frog starts on pad 189 and steps left to pad number 186, then to pad number 183, and continues leftward to pad 9 stepping only on every third pad. Daniel the toad starts on pad number 2 and steps up to pad number 6, then to pad number 10, and continues rightward to pad 198 stepping only on every fourth pad. How many pads were stepped on by both Dylan and Daniel (not necessarily at the same time)?
(A) 11
(B) 12
(C) 13
(D) 14
(E) 15

5. What is the remainder when 10987654321 is divided by 60?
(A) 1
(B) 2
(C) 3
(D) 4
(E) 5

6. What is the remainder when 2^{2021} is divided by 13?
(A) 2
(B) 4
(C) 6
(D) 8
(E) 10

7. A number is called special if it leaves a remainder of 200, 400, and 600 when divided by 900. How many special numbers are there between 900 and 9000?

(A) 24
(B) 27
(C) 30
(D) 33
(E) 36

8. What is the sum of the digits of the smallest positive integer greater than 1000 such that when it is divided by 13, the remainder is 11?

(A) 2
(B) 3
(C) 4
(D) 5
(E) 6

9. The product of two consecutive odd whole numbers is 255. The sum of the two numbers has n number of positive divisors. Find the value of n.

(A) 4
(B) 5
(C) 6
(D) 7
(E) 8

10. A positive integer is 3 more than a multiple of 13 and 4 more than a multiple of 17. Find the sum of the digits of the least integer it could be.

(A) 5
(B) 10
(C) 15
(D) 20
(E) 25

Answer Key from 1 to 10

1. (B)

Paraphrase $54 = kq + 5$ for some k and q. Then, $49 = kq$. Hence, $k = 1, 7, 49$. Since $k > 5$, there are two values of k. Hence, the answer is (B).

2. (C)

Notice that $27 \cdot 5 \equiv 3 \cdot 5 \equiv 3 \pmod{12}$. Hence, the answer must be March.

3. (D)

First, $5^2 \equiv 25 \equiv 1 \pmod{12}$, which is not "month equivalent." Keep continuing this process until we find out $9^2 \equiv 81 \equiv 9 \pmod{12}$. Hence, September is "month equivalent."

4. (E)

Let n be the pad number of lilypad. Then, Dylan must have reached $n \equiv 0 \pmod 3$, whereas Daniel must have stepped on $n \equiv 2 \pmod 4$. Let $n = 4k + 2$. Substitute it into the first modular equation, i.e., $4k + 2 \equiv 0 \pmod 3$. Hence, $k \equiv -2 \equiv 1 \pmod 3$, which implies $k = 3q + 1$ for some integer q. Substitute k into $n = 4k + 2$ to get $n = 4(3q+1) + 2 = 12q + 6$. Since $9 \leq n \leq 189$, there are 15 values of q, i.e, $q = 1, 2, \cdots, 15$. Hence, the answer is (E).

5. (A)

Let $n = 10987654321$. Then, $n \equiv 1 \pmod 4$, $n \equiv 1 \pmod 3$ and $n \equiv 1 \pmod 5$. It is not so challenging to see $n - 1 \equiv 0 \pmod{60}$. Hence, $n \equiv 1 \pmod{60}$. Thus, the answer is (A).

6. (C)

By Fermat's Little Theorem, $a^{p-1} \equiv 1 \pmod p$ where a is relatively prime to p and p is prime. In particular, $2^{12} \equiv 1 \pmod{13}$. Now, divide out 2021 by 12 to find out the remainder of 5, since $2021 = 12(168) + 5$. Hence, $2^{2021} \equiv 2^5 \equiv 32 \equiv 6 \pmod{13}$. Hence, the answer is (C).

7. (B)

Let n be such number. Then, $n = 900k + 200$, $n = 900k + 400$ or $n = 900k + 600$ for some integer k. Then, $900 < 900k + 200 < 9000$ implies that there exists 9 values of k. Similar process for other two cases shows that there exists 9 respective values of k. Therefore, there are 27 special numbers between 900 and 9000.

8. (C)

Paraphrase the condition into $n = 13k + 11$ for some k, or $n \equiv 11 \pmod{13}$. Since $13k + 11 > 1000$, bits of algebra tell us that $k > 76$. Hence, the smallest possible value of n equals $n = 13(77) + 11 = 1012$. The sum of the digits of 1012 is 4, so the answer is (C).

TOPIC_1 Divisor and Remainders

9. (C)

Let the larger odd number be $2k+1$. Then, the smaller odd must be $2k-1$. Hence, $(2k-1)(2k+1) = 255$ implies that $4k^2 = 256$. Thus, $k^2 = 64$ implies that $k = 8$, since they are whole numbers. The two numbers are 15 and 17, and the sum of the two results in $32(=2^5)$. Therefore, the number of positive divisors of 32 is $6(=\{1,2,4,8,16,32\})$.

10. (B)

Let the positive integer be n. Then, $n \equiv 3 \pmod{13}$ and $n \equiv 4 \pmod{17}$. First, $n = 17k + 4$. Then, $17k + 4 \equiv 3 \pmod{13}$. Thus, $17k \equiv -1 \pmod{13}$ implies that $4k \equiv 12 \pmod{13}$. Switch $k \equiv 3 \pmod{13}$ into $k = 13q + 3$, and put it into the original expression of n, i.e., $n = 17(13q + 3) + 4 = 221q + 55$. The smallest positive value of n is 55. Its digits' sum equals 10, so the answer is (B).

1.3 Prime Factorization

A natural number *n* always has a *unique* prime factorization, i.e.,

$$n = p_1^{q_1} p_2^{q_2} \cdots p_k^{q_k}$$

where $k \geq 1$ and $q_i \geq 0$ for all $i \in [1, k]$. A typical application of prime factorization consists of two parts : the *number of divisors* and *sum of divisors*. These sub-topics will covered in detail in later part of this book.

First, we must go over the question of what a prime number is. A prime number is a whole number whose only positive divisors consist of 1 and itself. In short, 2 is a prime, but 4 is not. In particular, a whole number that can be written as the product of two or more primes is known as "composite." Primes can also be categorized into

- 2 : the smallest even prime number (the only even prime).

- 3 : the smallest odd prime number.

- $6k \pm 1$: other prime numbers.

Now, if a whole number *n* is a composite number, then $n = ab$ for some *a*, *b* smaller than *n*. Assume $a \leq b$ without loss of generality. Then, $a^2 \leq n = ab$. Then, $a \leq \sqrt{n}$. If *a* were a prime divisor of *n*, then it must be at most the value of $\sqrt{n}$. This is quite useful for us to test whether a number is a prime or not.

Example Prime factorize 167.

Step-by-Step Solution
\# 1. Find all primes smaller than or equal to $\sqrt{167}$, i.e., $\{2, 3, 5, 7, 11\}$.
\# 2. Since none of the primes in the list divides 167, we conclude that 167 is a prime number.

Sometimes, it is useful for us to use the difference of squares, which is recommended for integers between 100 and 1,000. Have a look at the following example.

Example Prime factorize 187, using the difference of squares.

Step-by-Step Solution
\# 1. Notice that $187 = 196 - 9 = 14^2 - 3^2 = (14-3)(14+3) = 11 \cdot 17$.
\# 2. Of course, we could have used the property of multiples of 11.

In order to see whether a number is composite or prime, it may save some time if we know the properties of multiples of the first few primes.

- Multiples of 2 : the last digit is even number.

- Multiples of 3 : the sum of digits is divisible by 3.

- Multiples of 4 : the last two-digit is a multiple of 4.

- Multiples of 5 : the last digit is either 0 or 5.

- Multiples of 6 : multiples of both 2 and 3.

- Multiples of 8 : the last three-digit is a multiple of 8.

- Multiples of 9 : the sum of digits is divisible by 9.

- Multiples of 11 : the alternating sum of digits is divisible by 11. For instance, $165 = 1 - 6 + 5 = 11(0)$.

Example Show how 12345 is divisible by 3.

Step-by-Step Solution

\# 1.

$$\begin{aligned} 12345 &= 10000 + 2000 + 300 + 40 + 5 \\ &= (9999 + 1) + (2(999) + 2) + (3(99) + 3) + (4(9) + 4) + 5 \\ &\equiv 1 + 2 + 3 + 4 + 5 \pmod{3} \\ &\equiv 15 \pmod{3} \\ &\equiv 0 \pmod{3} \end{aligned}$$

\# 2. Since $9999 + 2(999) + 3(99) + 4(9)$ is divisible by 3 or 9, we simply look at $1 + 2 + 3 + 4 + 5 = 15$, which is also divisible by 3.

\# 3. We conclude that 12345 is divisible by 3.

Basic Drill 3

1. Prime factorize 2021.

2. Find the value of a if $\overline{1234a}$ is divisible by 9.

3. If $\overline{ab2}$ is a multiple of 11, how many ordered pairs of (a, b) are there?

4. Show that 2011 is a prime number.

Answer to Basic Drill 3

1.

$$2021 = 2025 - 4$$
$$= (45)^2 - (2)^2$$
$$= (45-2)(45+2)$$
$$= (43)(47)$$

Hence, $2021 = 43^1 \cdot 47^1$.

2.

Since the sum of digits of $1+2+3+4+a$ is divisible by 9, we conclude that $a+1$ is divisible by 9. Since $0 \leq a \leq 9$, we have $1 \leq a+1 \leq 10$. The only possible value of $a+1$ that is a multiple of 9 is 9. Hence, $a=8$.

3.

Since $a - b + 2 \equiv 0 \pmod{11}$, we notice that $a + 2 \equiv b \pmod{11}$. Hence, $(a,b) = (9,0)$, $(7,9)$, $(6,8)$, $(5,7)$, $(4,6)$, $(3,5)$, $(2,4)$, and $(1,3)$. Therefore, there are $\boxed{8}$ ordered pairs of (a,b).

4.

List all primes less than or equal to $\sqrt{2011} \approx 44.8$, i.e.,
$\{2, 3, 5, 7, 11, 13, 17, 19, 23, 29, 31, 37, 41, 43\}$. Manually check that there is no prime dividing 2011. Hence, we conclude that 2011 is a prime number.

Practice

11. What is the positive difference between the two largest prime factors of 159137?
(A) 6
(B) 12
(C) 14
(D) 20
(E) 26

12. If there are n positive factors of k, let's call it $f_1, f_2, f_3, \cdots, f_n$. On the other hand, $k = p_1^{a_1} p_2^{a_2} \cdots p_l^{a_l}$. Then,

$$\sum_{m=1}^{n} f_m = f_1 + f_2 + \cdots + f_n = \prod_{i=1}^{l} \left(\sum_{j=0}^{a_i} p_i^j \right) = (p_1^{a_1} + p_1^{a_1-1} + \cdots + 1)(p_2^{a_2} + p_2^{a_2-1} + \cdots + 1) \cdots$$

Which of the following is the sum of positive integer values of n such that $\dfrac{n+28}{n}$ is an integer?
(A) 52
(B) 54
(C) 56
(D) 58
(E) 60

13. For how many positive integer values of n will $n+1$ divide $n^3 + n^2 - n + 3$?

(A) 0
(B) 1
(C) 2
(D) 3
(E) 4

14. How many fractions in the form $\frac{n}{33}$, with $0 < n < 33$, are in lowest terms?

(A) 12
(B) 14
(C) 16
(D) 18
(E) 20

15. Find the number of all positive integers less than 2021 which are both multiples of 12 and one more than a multiple of 11.

(A) 14
(B) 16
(C) 18
(D) 20
(E) 22

16. Using $a^2 - b^2 = (a-b)(a+b)$, find the sum of distinct digits of the largest prime factor of 442.

(A) 2
(B) 4
(C) 6
(D) 8
(E) 10

17. For how many natural numbers less than 100 is the prime factorization containing two smallest primes only?

(A) 7
(B) 8
(C) 9
(D) 10
(E) 11

18. Let N equal the product of all counting numbers from 1 through 2021:

$$N = 1 \times 2 \times 3 \times 4 \times \cdots \times 2021.$$

How many terminal zeros will N have when it is written in standard form?

(A) 501
(B) 502
(C) 503
(D) 504
(E) 505

19. The number 1000! has a long tail of zeroes. How many zeroes are there? (Reminder: The number $n!$ is the product of the integers from 1 to n. For example, $5! = 5 \cdot 4 \cdot 3 \cdot 2 \cdot 1 = 120$.)

(A) 247
(B) 248
(C) 249
(D) 250
(E) 251

20. Let $k = 2 \cdot 5 \cdot 8 \cdots 98 \cdot 101$. Find the number of terminal zeros of the decimal representation of k.

(A) 2
(B) 4
(C) 6
(D) 8
(E) 10

Answer Key from 11 to 20

11. (C)

Since $159137 = 11 \cdot 17 \cdot 23 \cdot 37$, we find out the two largest prime factors are 23 and 37. Hence, the difference is 14.

12. (C)

Since $\frac{n+28}{n} = 1 + \frac{28}{n}$ is an integer, n must divide out 28. Hence, n must be a divisor of 28. Therefore, $n = 1, 2, 4, 7, 14, 28$. In conclusion, the sum of all possible n values is $1 + 2 + 4 + 7 + 14 + 28 = 56$.

13. (C)

Since $n^3 + n - n + 3 = (n+1)(n^2 - 1) + 4$, 4 must be divisible by $n+1$. Therefore, $n + 1 = 1, 2, 4$, i.e., $n = 0, 1, 3$. Since n must be positive, there are 2 values of n.

14. (E)

We must find out integers from 1 to 32, inclusive, such that they are "relatively prime" to 33. This brings forth "Euler's Totient function," which uses the principle of inclusion and exclusion, also known as P.I.E. In particular,

$$\phi(33) = 33(1 - \frac{1}{3})(1 - \frac{1}{11})$$
$$= 33(1 - \frac{1}{3} - \frac{1}{11} + \frac{1}{33})$$
$$= 33 - 11 - 3 + 1$$
$$= 20$$

This is indeed the application of P.I.E, i.e.,

$$n(A \cup B)^c = n(U) - (n(A) + n(B) - n(A \cap B))$$
$$= n(U) - n(A) - n(B) + n(A \cap B)$$

where U is the universal set containing both A and B.

15. (B)

Let n be such number. Then, $n \equiv 0 \pmod{12}$ and $n = \equiv 1 \pmod{11}$. First, $12k \equiv 1 \pmod{11}$, so $k \equiv 1 \pmod{11}$. In short, $k = 11q + 1$. Finally, $n = 12k = 12(11q + 1) = 132q + 12$. Since $132q + 12 < 2021$, we get $q \leq 15$. Hence, $n = 12, 12 + 132, 12 + 2(132), \cdots, 12 + 15(132)$ implies that there are 16 n-values.

16. (D)

First, $442 = 2 \cdot 221$. Notice that $221 = 225 - 4 = 15^2 - 2^2 = (15 - 2)(15 + 2) = 13 \cdot 17$. Hence, the greatest prime factor is 17. The sum of its distinct digits is 8.

17. (C)

Let $n = 2^p 3^q$ where $p, q \geq 1$. If $p = 1$, then $n = 2 \cdot 3^q < 100$ implies $q = 1, 2, 3$. If $p = 2$, then $n = 4 \cdot 3^q < 100$ implies that $q = 1, 2$. If $p = 3$, then $n = 8 \cdot 3^q < 100$ implies that $q = 1, 2$. If $p = 4$, then $n = 16 \cdot 3^q < 100$ implies that $q = 1$. If $p = 5$, then $n = 32 \cdot 3^q < 100$ implies that $q = 1$. Therefore, there are 9 values of n.

18. (C)

Terminal zeros are determined by the number of 2's and that of 5's. As one can expect, there must be less number of 5's in 2021!. Hence, let's capture the number of 5's in 2021! by using Legendre's symbol.

$$\lfloor \frac{2021}{5} \rfloor + \lfloor \frac{2021}{25} \rfloor + \lfloor \frac{2021}{125} \rfloor + \lfloor \frac{2021}{625} \rfloor = 404 + 80 + 16 + 3 = 503$$

19. (C)

Apply same tactic as we did in 18. Let's use Legendre's symbol.

$$\lfloor \frac{1000}{5} \rfloor + \lfloor \frac{1000}{25} \rfloor + \lfloor \frac{1000}{125} \rfloor + \lfloor \frac{1000}{625} \rfloor = 200 + 40 + 8 + 1 = 249$$

20. (D)

Let each number that appears in the product as n. Then, $n = 3k + 2$ for some integer k. We would like to find out whether $n \equiv 0 \pmod{5}$, as we did in question 18 and 19. Hence, $3k + 2 \equiv 0 \pmod{5}$ implies that $3k \equiv 3 \pmod{5}$, so $k \equiv 1 \pmod{5}$. Therefore, $n = 5, 20, 35, 50, 65, 80$ and 95. All values of n other than $n = 50$ contain only one multiple of 5, whereas 50 contains two 5's. Therefore, there are 8 number of 5's in the list, so there are 8 terminal zeros.

Did you know?

1. Babylonians in 1600 BC were capable of solving "Pythagorean equation" using only integers.

2. Pythagoras and his school around 500 BC already knew how to solve Pythagorean equation $a^2 + b^2 = c^2$ using integers.

3. Euclid in 300 BC already dealt with prime factorization.

4. Diophantus of Alexandria around 250 AD influenced in great amount in Number Theory.

5. Around 1637, Fermat came up with his last theorem, $a^n + b^n = c^n$ has no positive integers a, b, c satisfying the equation if $n \geq 3$, which is proved by Professor Andrew Wiles in 1994.

6. Legendre wrote the first textbook on Number Theory in 1798.

7. Carl Gauss wrote the famous "Disquisitiones Arithmeticae" in 1801, describing Number Theory as the Queen of Mathematics.

8. Dirichlet wrote in his memoir that $ax + b$ where a and b are relatively prime represents a prime number for some integer x. He proved it using "analysis" tools - limits and continuity, hence making a foundation for "analytic number theory."

9. In 1742, Goldbach wrote a letter to Euler, proposing many conjectures, including one suggesting that an even number can always be written as the sum of two primes. This conjecture, although considered true, has not been proved yet.

10. There are hundreds of unsolved Number Theory questions, including ones proposed by Goldbach.

TOPIC 2

Least Common Multiple and Greatest Common Divisor

2.1 Least Common Multiple

Given two positive integers a and b, we find the least common multiple using two methods. The first method uses prime factorization. Instead of getting our investigation into abstract level, let's go over with simpler examples and learn how to compute the least common multiple.

Example Compute the least common multiple of 52 and 42.

Step-by-Step Solution
#1. $52 = 2^2 \cdot 13$ and $42 = 2 \cdot 3 \cdot 7$.
#2. Choose the maximum exponents of primes that appeared at least once.
#3. $2^2 \cdot 3 \cdot 7 \cdot 13$ is the least common multiple.

As one can notice, the least common multiple takes in whichever that appears at least once and maximum exponents of the common primes.

Another way of finding the least common multiple can be found by writing a and b as gx and gy where g is the greatest common divisor, and x, y are relatively prime. The least common multiple, in fact, can be written as gxy.

Example Compute the least common multiple of 12 and 18.

Step-by-Step Solution
#1. Since the greatest common divisor of two numbers is 6, let $12 = 6(2)$ and $18 = 6(3)$.
#2. Hence, the least common multiple can be written as $36 = gxy$ where $g = 2$, $x = 2$, and $y = 3$.
#3. Notice that 2 and 3 are relatively prime.

Using the same g to express a and b, i.e., $a = gx$ and $b = gy$, the following property always holds true : the product of a and b is the product of the greatest common divisor and the least common multiple.

$$a \cdot b = g \cdot (gxy)$$

Example If the product of a and b, where a and b are two relatively prime positive integers, equals 36, find the number of pairs (a, b).

Step-by-Step Solution
#1. Notice that $a = 1(x)$ and $b = 1(y)$ where x and y are relatively prime.
#2. Prime factorize 36 into $2^2 \cdot 3^2$.
#3. There are two slots for 2^2 to choose. Also, there are the same number of slots for 3^2 to be choose.
#4. There are 4 possible pairs (a, b), i.e., $(1, 36)$, $(4, 9)$, $(9, 4)$ and $(36, 1)$.

Basic Drill 4

1. Find the least common multiple of 7, 11, 13, and 1001.

2. If a and b are relatively prime positive integers, whose product equals 1001, find the value of least common multiple of a and b.

3. If a and b are relatively prime positive integers, whose product equals 1001, find the number of ordered pairs (a, b).

4. If the product of two positive integers m and n is 8, find the sum of all possible least common multiples of m and n.

Answer to Basic Drill 4

1.
Notice that $1001 = 7 \times 11 \times 13$. Therefore, the least common multiple of 7, 11, 13, and 1001 must be $\boxed{1001}$.

2.
Since $ab = 1001 = 7 \cdot 11 \cdot 13$, and $a = 1(x)$ and $b = 1(y)$ where x and y are relatively prime, the least common multiple of a and b can be written as $1xy$, which equals ab. Therefore, the least common multiple must be $\boxed{1001}$.

3.
Since $ab = 1001 = 7 \cdot 11 \cdot 13$, where a and b are relative prime, we can use the rule of counting to find out the number of ordered pairs (a, b). First, let's have a look at 7. Since a and b are relatively prime, 7 can be placed either at a or b. In other words, there are 2 possible choices. Second, 11 also has two places to choose. Likewise, 13 has two spots to choose. In particular, $(a, b) = (1, 1001), (7, 143), (11, 91), (13, 77), (77, 13), (91, 11), (143, 7)$, and $(1001, 1)$. Hence, there are $\boxed{8}$ number of ordered pairs (a, b).

4.
Let g be the greatest common divisor of m and n. Then, $mn = g(gxy)$ where $m = gx$ and $n = gy$, assuming that x and y are relatively prime positive integers. Then, $mn = g^2 xy$ implies that $g^2 = 1$ and 4. First, if $g = 1$, then $xy = 8$, implying that $(x, y) = (8, 1), (1, 8)$. Therefore, the least common multiple of m and n is 8. Second, if $g = 2$, then $xy = 2$, implying that $(x, y) = (2, 1), (1, 2)$. Hence, the least common multiple of m and n is 4. Therefore, the sum of all possible least common multiples of m and n is $\boxed{12}$.

Practice

1. How many positive integers, not exceeding 100, are relatively prime to 6 or 14?
(A) 45
(B) 46
(C) 47
(D) 48
(E) 49

2. Two circles, one of radius 10 centimeters, the other of radius 6 centimeters, are externally tangent at point P marked with a distinct color. If *P* moves along the larger circle counterclockwise with the speed of 6π centimeters per minute, and it moves along the other circle clockwise with the speed of 5π centimeters per minute, how many minutes will pass before the marks coincide with one another for the first time other than the beginning coincidence?
(A) 15
(B) 30
(C) 45
(D) 60
(E) 75

3. There are two gears of different sizes. The left gear turns 32 times in a minute, whereas the right gear turns 54 times in a minute. Initially, the leftgear has a mark due west, while the rightgear has a mark due east. After how many seconds will the two gears next have both their marks pointing the original direction altogether?

(A) 10

(B) 15

(C) 30

(D) 36

(E) 72

4. A group of 60 students, including Abby, Bob, Claire, and David, cooked up a large positive integer. "It can be divided by 1," said Abby for the first time. "It can be divided by 2," said Bob afterwards. "And by 3," continued Claire. "And by 4," added David. This continued until everyone had made such comment with one larger integer at a time. If exactly two friends who said consecutive integers were wrong, what are the largest possible sum of these two numbers?

(A) 55

(B) 57

(C) 59

(D) 61

(E) 63

40 The Essential Guide to **Competition Math** [Number Theory]

5. Bob and Bo each selected a positive integer less than 1000. Bob's number is a multiple of 24, and Bo's number is a multiple of 32. If the probability that they selected the same number can be written as m/n where m and n are relatively prime, compute the sum $m + n$.
(A) 1247
(B) 1253
(C) 1269
(D) 1281
(E) 1291

6. Which of the following is the sum of exponents of the largest square that divides the least common multiple of 18, 24, and 100?
(A) 0
(B) 2
(C) 4
(D) 6
(E) 8

7. If the product of two positive integers is 264 where the two integers are not relatively prime, find the smallest value of their sum.

(A) 32
(B) 34
(C) 36
(D) 38
(E) 40

8. If two positive integers m and n have the least common multiple of 30, find the number of all possible ordered pairs (m, n).

(A) 24
(B) 27
(C) 30
(D) 33
(E) 36

9. The least common multiple of x, 20 and 28 is 140. Find the number of all possible integer values of x, assuming that x is greater than or equal to 1.
(A) 11
(B) 12
(C) 13
(D) 14
(E) 15

10. If an integer is divisible by 11, but leaves a remainder of 1 when divided by any integer 2 through 10, find the sum of the digits of least possible positive integer.
(A) 10
(B) 11
(C) 12
(D) 13
(E) 14

Answer Key from 1 to 10

1. (D)

First, let A be the set of multiples of 2, B the set of multiples of 3, and C the set of multiples of 7, all of which has a number smaller than or equal to 100. Now, let's paraphrase "relatively prime to 6 or 14" into a mathematical statement, i.e.,

$$(A^c \cap B^c) \cup (A^c \cap C^c) = A^c \cap (B^c \cup C^c)$$

By De Morgan's law, we convert the last expression into $(A \cup (B \cap C))^c$. In other words, we compute the complement of $A \cup (B \cap C)$.

$$100 - \left(\lfloor \frac{100}{2} \rfloor + \lfloor \frac{100}{21} \rfloor - \lfloor \frac{100}{42} \rfloor\right) = 100 - (50 + 4 - 2) = 100 - 52 = 48$$

2. (D)

For the larger circle, it takes 20/6 minutes to complete 1 rotation. Likewise, for the smaller circle, it takes 12/5 minutes to complete 1 rotation. In other words, the larger circle rotates 6/20 amount per minute, whereas the smaller one 5/12 amount per minute. Hence, we must make $6t/20 (= 3t/10)$ and $5t/12$ both whole numbers after t minutes of rotation. In short, we must produce the least common multiple of 12 and 10. The answer must be (D).

3. (C)

The left gear rotates 32/60 amount per second. Likewise, the right gear rotates 54/60 amount per second. After t seconds, each one rotates $8t/15$ amount and $9t/10$ amount, respectively. Since the least common multiple of 15 and 10 are 30, the answer must be (C).

4. (E)

We must investigate all the primes and integers next to these primes. Notice that if a student says 31, then the number is not divisible by 31. This may be true because there is no other prime number other than 31 nor multiples of 31 that appeared in the list to divide out 31. If another student says 32, then the number is not divisible by 32. There are 5 number of 2's. The only number that we need is a multiple of 32 to come out in the list so that the large number is divisible by 32. However, the next multiple of 32 (=64) does not show up in the list. Therefore, 31 and 32 are such numbers. The answer is (E).

5. (D)

First, there are $\lfloor \frac{999}{24} \rfloor$ number of multiples of 24 less than or equal to 999. Likewise, there are $\lfloor \frac{999}{32} \rfloor$ number of multiples of 32 less than or equal to 999. Since the least common multiple of 24 and 32 are 96, and there are 10 multiples of 96 less than or equal to 999, we conclude that $\frac{m}{n} = \frac{10}{41 \cdot 31} = \frac{10}{1271}$. Hence, the answer must be (D).

6. (D)

Notice that $18 = 2 \cdot 3^2$, $24 = 2^3 \cdot 3$ and $100 = 2^2 \cdot 5^2$. Therefore, the least common multiple of these numbers is $2^3 \cdot 3^2 \cdot 5^2$. The largest square that divides this value must be $2^2 \cdot 3^2 \cdot 5^2$. Therefore, the sum of the exponents is 6. The answer is (D).

7. (B)

Let a and b be the two positive integers. Then, $a \cdot b = g^2 xy$ where g is the greatest common divisor, and x and y are relatively prime. According to the given question, we notice that $g = 2$. Therefore, $a = 2x$ and $b = 2y$. Thus, $xy = 2 \cdot 3 \cdot 11$. In order to minimize the sum of a and b, we need to let $(x, y) = (6, 11)$ or $(11, 6)$. Thus, $a + b = 2(x + y) = 2(17) = 34$. The answer is (B).

8. (B)

Let $m = gx$ and $n = gy$ for the greatest common divisor g where x and y are relatively prime. Since $gxy = 2 \cdot 3 \cdot 5$. There are two ways of explaining why there are 27 pairs of (m, n). Let's go over the first method. Since 2, 3, and 5 have three places, i.e., $\{g, x, y\}$ to choose, there are $3^3 (= 27)$ number of $(m, n) = (gx, gy)$. The second method is case enumeration. If $g = 1$, then there are $2^3 = 8$ ways of sending 2, 3, and 5 to x and y. If $g = 2$, then there are $2^2 = 4$ ways of sending 3 and 5 to x and y.

9. (B)

Notice that $20 = 2^2 \cdot 5$, $28 = 2^2 \cdot 7$, and $140 = 2^2 \cdot 5 \cdot 7$. Then, let $x = 2^a 5^b 7^c$ where a, b, and c are whole numbers. Since $0 \le a \le 2$, $0 \le b \le 1$ and $0 \le c \le 1$, we have $12 (= 3 \cdot 2 \cdot 2)$ possibilities. The answer is (B).

10. (A)

Let this integer be n. Then, $n \equiv 1$ (mod lcm of $2, 3, 4, 5, 6, 7, 8, 9, 10$). Hence, $n \equiv 1$ (mod 2520). Now, $n = 2520k + 1$ for some integer k. Since $n \equiv 0$ (mod 11), we solve $2520k + 1 \equiv 0$ (mod 11) to get $k \equiv 10$ (mod 11). Substituting $k = 10$ to get $n = 25201$, we conclude that 25201 is the smallest positive integer satisfying the given condition. Hence, the answer is (A).

2.2 Greatest Common Divisor

Given two positive integers a and b, we find the greatest common divisor using two methods. The first method uses prime factorization. Instead of getting our investigation into abstract level, let's go over with simpler examples and learn how to compute the greatest common divisor.

Example Compute the greatest common divisor of 52 and 42.

Step-by-Step Solution
#1. $52 = 2^2 \cdot 13$ and $42 = 2 \cdot 3 \cdot 7$.
#2. Choose the minimum exponents of the common primes between the two.
#3. 2 is the greatest common divisor.

Unlike "least common multiple," the greatest common divisor takes the minimum exponents of the common primes. Another way of finding the greatest common divisor can be found by writing a and b as gx and gy where g is the greatest common divisor, and x, y are relatively prime. Given $a = gx$ and $b = gy$, the following property always holds true : the product of a and b is the product of the greatest common divisor and the least common multiple. Restating this, we find out that the greatest common divisor equals the fraction when the product of a and b is divided by their least common multiple.

$$\frac{a \cdot b}{gxy} = g \longleftrightarrow a \cdot b = g^2 xy$$

Example If the product of a and b, where a and b are not relatively prime positive integers, equals 36, find the number of pairs (a, b).

Step-by-Step Solution
#1. Notice that $a = gx$ and $b = gy$ where x and y are relatively prime.
#2. Since $ab = g^2 xy$ and $g \neq 1$, by the original assumption, we know that $g = 2, 3, 6$.
#3. If $g = 2$, then $(x, y) = (1, 9), (3, 3), (9, 1)$.
#4. If $g = 3$, then $(x, y) = (1, 4), (2, 2), (4, 1)$.
#5. If $g = 6$, then $(x, y) = (1, 1)$.
#6. Since there are some duplicates $(a, b) = (6, 6)$, we get rid of $(x, y) = (2, 2)$ and $(x, y) = (1, 1)$ when $g = 3$ and $g = 6$, respectively.
#7. Hence, there are 5 possible pairs of (a, b).

Basic Drill 5

1. Find the greatest common divisor of 154 and 1012.

2. If the greatest common divisor of 14! and p^n is 1024, find the value of p and n, where p is prime.

3. If $a \cdot b = 2^2 \cdot 3^2 \cdot 5^2 \cdot 7^2 \cdot 11^2$, where a and b are relatively prime positive integers, find the number of ordered pairs (a, b).

4. If the product of two positive integers m and n is 441, find the sum of all possible greatest common divisors of m and n.

Answer to Basic Drill 5

1.
First, $154 = 11 \cdot 14$ and $1012 = 11 \cdot 92$. Since 14 and 92 are even numbers, but not multiples of 4, we conclude that the greatest common divisor of 154 and 1012 is $\boxed{22}$.

2.
First, $14! = 2^{11} \cdot K$ for some odd integer K. The greatest common factor is $1024(= 2^{10})$, so p^n must have ten number 2's in its prime factorization. Since p is a prime number, we notice that p^n is the unique prime factorization of p^n, and $p = 2$. We can conclude that $n = 10$. Hence, $\boxed{(p, n) = (2, 10)}$.

3.
Since a and b are relatively prime, 2^2 must be placed in either at a or b. Similar placements should be made for 3^2, 5^2, 7^2 and 11^2. Hence, there are $\boxed{32}$ possible ordered pairs of (a, b).

4.
Let g be the greatest common divisor of m and n. Then, $mn = g(gxy)$ where $m = gx$ and $n = gy$, assuming that x and y are relatively prime positive integers. Then, $mn = g^2xy$ implies that $g^2 = 1, 9, 49, 441$. Hence, $g = 1, 3, 7$ and 21. Thus, the sum of all possible greatest common divisors of m and n is $\boxed{32}$.

Practice

11. Two entomologists agree that rare hornets are worth $520 and rare mantis worth $858. If the two exchange some of their hornets and mantis for economic transaction, due to their love of insects, what could be the value of financial amount if they liquidate their assets?

(A) 282
(B) 284
(C) 286
(D) 288
(E) 290

12. The three consecutive odd digits a, b, and c are used to form the three-digit numbers $\overline{abc}$ and $\overline{cba}$. What is the sum of the digits of the greatest common divisor of all numbers of the form $\overline{abc} + \overline{cba}$?

(A) 3
(B) 6
(C) 9
(D) 12
(E) 15

TOPIC_2 Least Common Multiple and Greatest Common Divisor

13. Assume that the arithmetic sequence $\{a_n\}$ can have negative, 0 and positive indices. If a_1 of the arithmetic sequence is -30 and the common difference d is a natural number, find the number of possible values of d if there exists some integer k such that $a_k + a_{k+5} = 0$.
(A) 2
(B) 3
(C) 4
(D) 5
(E) 6

14. What is the sum of the digits of the largest prime that must divide the sum of the first 2021 terms of any arithmetic sequence whose least terms is at least 1?
(A) 7
(B) 9
(C) 11
(D) 13
(E) 15

15. September 23 is a "relatively prime date" since the greatest common factor of 9 and 23 is 1, i.e., 9 and 23 are relatively prime. What is the sum of all possible relatively prime dates in February of any year?
(A) 27
(B) 29
(C) 31
(D) 33
(E) 35

16. Which of the following is a multiple of the greatest common divisor of 221 and 323?
(A) 26
(B) 34
(C) 38
(D) 39
(E) 57

17. What is the sum of the digits of the least integer greater than 1000 for which the greatest common factor of that integer and 30 is 3?

(A) 3
(B) 6
(C) 9
(D) 12
(E) 15

18. If 1989 is split into 198 and 9, then the two integers, 198 and 9, are not relatively prime. How many odd-numbered year between 2000 and 2020 satisfy this property?

(A) 1
(B) 2
(C) 3
(D) 4
(E) 5

19. If $a \cdot b = 10!$ and their greatest common divisor is the second smallest perfect square that divides 10!, compute the number of all possible pairs (a, b).

(A) 8
(B) 10
(C) 12
(D) 14
(E) 16

20. What is the sum of the exponents the largest perfect square that divides the greatest common divisor of 50! and $2^3 3^4 4^5 5^6 6^7 7^8 8^9 9^{10}$?

(A) 78
(B) 80
(C) 82
(D) 84
(E) 86

Answer Key from 11 to 20

11. (C)
By Bezout's identity, $520x + 858y$ is a multiple of the greatest common divisor of 520 and 858, i.e., 26. In fact, $|520x + 858y| = 26k$ for some integer k. Hence, find a multiple of 26 in the answer choice. The answer must be (C).

12. (B)
Since $\overline{abc} + \overline{cba} = 666$, 1110, or 1554, the greatest common divisor of these three numbers is 222. Therefore, the sum of digits must be 6. The answer must be (B).

13. (C)
Since $a_k + a_{k+5} = 0$ can be paraphrased into $-30 + (k-1)d - 30 + (k+4)d = 0$, we can conclude that $60 = 2kd + 3d = (2k+3)d$. Since $2k+3$ is always an odd number, we can find $2k + 3 = 1, 3, 5, 15$. Hence, there are 4 values of d. The answer is (C).

14. (C)
Notice that $a_1 + a_2 + \cdots + a_{2021} = \frac{2021(2a_1 + 2020d)}{2} = 2021(a_1 + 1010d)$. This implies that the greatest common divisor must be 2021, and $2021 = 43 \cdot 47$. Hence, the largest prime divisor must be 47. Therefore, the answer must be (C).

15. (B)
In a leap year, February has 29 days. Odd dates must be relatively prime, so there are 15 dates. Likewise, in a non-leap year, February has 28 days. There are only 14 odd dates. Hence, the sum must be 29. The answer is (B).

16. (B)
Since $221 = 225 - 4 = 15^2 - 2^2 = (13)(17)$ and $323 = 324 - 1 = 18^2 - 1^2 = (17)(19)$, we get the greatest common divisor of 17. Out of answer choices, (B) is the only multiple of 17. Hence, the answer must be (B).

17. (A)
First, 1002 is a multiple of 6, so it contradicts the given condition. Second, 1005 is a multiple of 15, so it also contradicts the given condition. Third, 1008 is also even. The least number that works is 1011 which is a multiple of 3 and 337. Hence, the answer is (A).

18. (C)
Out of $\{2001, 2003, 2005, 2007, 2009, 2011, 2013, 2015, 2017, 2019\}$, there are 2005, 2013, and 2019 that satisfy the given property. Hence, the answer is (C).

54 The Essential Guide to **Competition Math** [Number Theory]

19. (E)

Since $10! = 2^8 \cdot 3^4 \cdot 5^2 \cdot 7^1$, and the greatest common divisor is 4, we conclude that $a = 4x$ and $b = 4y$ where x and y are relatively prime. Hence, 2^4, 3^4, 5^2 and 7^1 all have two slots in which they can be placed, so there are $16 (= 2^4)$ number of (a, b)'s. In fact, this is a concept of binomial expression. We simply look at the number of cases to place 2^4, 3^4, 5^2, and 7^1 into a or b. Therefore, the answer is (E).

20. (C)

Notice that $2^3 \cdot 3^4 \cdot 4^5 \cdot 5^6 \cdot 6^7 \cdot 7^8 \cdot 8^9 \cdot 9^{10}$ can be factorized into $2^{47} \cdot 3^{31} \cdot 5^6 \cdot 7^8$. Similarly, $50!$ can be factorized into $2^{47} \cdot 3^{22} \cdot 5^{12} \cdot 7^8 \cdots 41 \cdot 43 \cdot 47$. Since the greatest common divisor only takes in the common divisors, we conlcude that it consists of 2, 3, 5, and 7 only. Taking the minimum exponents of the two expressions, we find out the value of greatest common divisor, i.e., $2^{47} \cdot 3^{22} \cdot 5^6 \cdot 7^8$. Hence, the largest perfect square that divides this number is $2^{46} \cdot 3^{22} \cdot 5^6 \cdot 7^8$. The sum of the exponents is $46 + 22 + 6 + 8 = 82$. The answer must be (C).

2.3 Eulidean Algorithm and Bezout's Identity

Euclidean Algorithm is a great way to find the greatest common divisor of two "large" integers, especially when it is difficult to prime factorize the given integers.

First, given two positive integers a_1, a_2, let's assume that $a_1 \geq a_2$. Then, there exists some unique (q_1, a_3) such that $a_1 = a_2 q_1 + a_3$ where $0 \leq a_3 < a_2$, by division algorithm. Euclidean algorithm, in fact, tells us that $\gcd(a_1, a_2) = \gcd(a_2, a_3)$. We keep continuing this procedure until we reach some integer k such that $\gcd(a_k, 0)$ is reached. We say, a_k is the greatest common divisor of a_1 and a_2.

$$\begin{aligned}\gcd(a_1, a_2) &= \gcd(a_2, a_3) \\ &= \gcd(a_3, a_4) \\ &= \gcd(a_4, a_5) \\ &= \gcd(a_5, a_6) \\ &= \vdots \\ &= \gcd(a_k, 0) \\ &= a_k\end{aligned}$$

Example Compute the greatest common divisor of $3^{15} + 3^8 + 1$ and $3^5 - 1$.

Step-by-Step Solution
#1. Notice that $3^{15} + 3^8 + 1$ is quite large.
#2. Hence, use Euclidean Algorithm by labeling $a_1 = 3^{15} + 3^8 + 1$ and $a_2 = 3^5 - 1$.
#3. $\gcd(3^{15} + 3^8 + 1, 3^5 - 1) = \gcd(3^5 - 1, 3^3 + 2)$
#4. $\gcd(3^5 - 1, 3^3 + 2) = \gcd(3^3 + 2, -2 \cdot 3^2 - 1)$
#5. $\gcd(29, -19) = 1$. Hence, the greatest common divisor of the original two numbers is 1.

The idea of using Euclidean algorithm is not limited to comparing two numbers. It can be used to polynomial expression as well.

Example Find the largest possible greatest common divisor of $15x - 7$ and $3x + 1$ where x is any integer.

Step-by-Step Solution
#1. $\gcd(15x - 7, 3x + 1) = \gcd(3x + 1, -12) = \gcd(3x + 1, |-12|)$.
#2. Then, there are six possible values of greatest common divisor, i.e., 1, 2, 3, 4, 6, and 12.
#3. Notice that $3x + 1$ has the reaminder of 1 when divided by 3. The largest possible value that satisfies this condition is 4.

Now, we should discuss the basic format of Bezout's identity. This can be combined with Euclidean algorithm to apply the concept of greatest common divisor in problem-solving. In fact, a question number 11 in topic 2 is using Bezout's identity. Here goes the theorem.

If a and b are integers not both equal to 0, then there exist some integers x and y such that $\gcd(a, b) = ax + by$, where $\gcd(a, b)$ is the greatest common divisor of a and b.

Example Find the smallest possible positive integer that can be expressed as the sum of multiples of 12 and 18.

Step-by-Step Solution
#1. Let $n = 12x + 18y$ for some integers x and y.
#2. $12x + 18y = 6(2x + 3y)$. Since 2 and 3 are relatively prime, we conclude that $n = 12x + 18y = 6(2x + 3y) = 6k$ for some integer k.
#3. Hence, we conclude that the smallest possible value that can be expressed as the sum of multiples of 12 and 18 is 6.

Now, if we allow non-negative integers only for x and y, then $ax + by$ where a and b are relatively prime positive integers, the largest integer that cannot be written as a linear combination of a and b is $ab - a - b$, which is known as "Chicken McNugget Theorem." According to the source in *Art of Problem Solving* website, the theorem originated from customers at McDonald's, where it sold its nuggets in packs of 9 and 20, and math-loving customers came up with conclusion that they cannot buy $151 (= 9 \cdot 20 - 9 - 20)$ nuggets even if they wanted to.

Basic Drill 6

1. Use Euclidean algorithm to find out the greatest common divisor of 1742 and 1781.

2. Find the smallest positive integer that can be written in the form of $2021a + 817b$ where a and b are integers.

3. As n ranges over integers greater than 5, find the maximum possible value of the greatest common divisor of $12n + 5$ and $5n + 1$.

4. Find the greatest common divisor of $3^{10} - 1$ and $3^4 - 1$.

Answer to Basic Drill 6

1.

$$\begin{aligned} \gcd(1781, 1742) &= \gcd(1742, 39) \\ &= \gcd(39, 26) \\ &= \gcd(26, 13) \\ &= \gcd(13, 0) \end{aligned}$$

Hence, the greatest common divisor is $\boxed{13}$.

2.

$$\begin{aligned} \gcd(2021, 817) &= \gcd(817, 387) \\ &= \gcd(387, 43) \\ &= \gcd(43, 0) \end{aligned}$$

Hence, the greatest common divisor of 2021 and 817 is 43. Therefore, $2021a + 817b = 43(47a + 19b)$. By Bezout's identity, we know that $47a + 19b = 1$ is true for some (a, b). In fact, if $(a, b) = (17, -42)$, $47a + 19b = 1$. Thus, the smallest positive integer that can be written as $2021a + 817b$ is $\boxed{43}$.

3.

$$\begin{aligned} \gcd(12n + 5, 5n + 1) &= \gcd(5n + 1, 2n + 3) \\ &= \gcd(2n + 3, n - 5) \\ &= \gcd(n - 5, 13) \end{aligned}$$

Depending on the value of n, the greatest common divisor might be 1 or 13. The largest possible value is $\boxed{13}$.

4.

$$\begin{aligned} \gcd(3^{10} - 1, 3^4 - 1) &= \gcd(3^4 - 1, 3^2 - 1) \\ &= \gcd(3^2 - 1, 0) \end{aligned}$$

This implies that the greatest common divisor of $3^{10} - 1$ and $3^4 - 1$ is $\boxed{8}$.

Practice

21. Suppose that p and q are positive integers such that $p - q = 10$ and $\gcd\left(\dfrac{p^3 + q^3}{p + q}, pq\right) = 25$. Which of the following is the sum of digits of p and q for smallest possible value of q?

(A) 5

(B) 7

(C) 9

(D) 11

(E) 13

22. Given x is a two-digit integer, which of the following is the largest possible value for the greatest common divisor between $(x + 27)(x + 37)$ and x?

(A) 9

(B) 27

(C) 37

(D) 64

(E) 99

23. If $f(x) = x^2 - x + 2020$, then what is the greatest common divisor of $f(201)$ and $f(200)$?

(A) 2
(B) 5
(C) 10
(D) 20
(E) 40

24. Let g be the greatest common divisor of $2^{1001} - 1$ and $2^{2015} - 1$. If the prime factorization of g can be written as $p_1^{a_1} p_2^{a_2} \cdots p_k^{a_k}$ where $k \geq 1$, then which of the following equals the following sum, provided that $S(n)$ is the sum of the digits of n?

$$\sum_{i=1}^{k} S(p_i)$$

(A) 18
(B) 19
(C) 20
(D) 21
(E) 22

25. Find the greatest common divisor of 999 and 1156324.(Hint : $999 = 27 \cdot 37$.)

(A) 13
(B) 27
(C) 37
(D) 601
(E) 999

26. Let $f(n) = 23n + 13$ and $g(n) = 7n - 4$ where n is a positive integer greater than 79. If $h(n)$ is the greatest common divisor between $f(n)$ and $g(n)$, which of the following is the sum of all possible values of $h(n)$?

(A) 3
(B) 61
(C) 122
(D) 248
(E) 288

27. Find out the sum of the digits of the smallest possible whole number n such that $n = 1001a + 3927b$ where a and b are integers.

(A) 4
(B) 7
(C) 14
(D) 17
(E) 20

28. What is the greatest common divisor of $2^{297} - 1$ and $2^{288} - 1$?

(A) 63
(B) 127
(C) 255
(D) 511
(E) 1023

29. Let a, b, c, and d are integers. If $1150a + 320b + 30c + 2d = 1096$, then find the smallest possible value of $|475a + 100b + 15c + d|$.

(A) 8
(B) 12
(C) 20
(D) 28
(E) 32

30. Given an integer n and m, which of the following is the smallest possible positive integer that can be expressed as the following absoluted-valued difference of n and m?

$$\left| n \times \left(\sum_{i=1}^{10} i^4 \right) - 1001 \times m \right| = |n \times (1^4 + 2^4 + 3^4 + \cdots + 10^4) - 1001m|$$

(A) 18
(B) 28
(C) 54
(D) 65
(E) 77

Answer Key from 21 to 30

21. (D)

First, $\frac{p^3+q^3}{p+q}$ can be rewritten as $p^2 - pq + q^2$. Then, it is not so difficult to check $\gcd(p^2 - pq + q^2, pq) = \gcd(pq, (p-q)^2)$ by Euclidean Algorithm. Hence, $\gcd(pq, 100) = 25$. Hence, $pq = 25(2k+1)$ for some $k \geq 0$. Otherwise, $pq = 50k$, so $\gcd(pq, 100) = 50$, which contradicts the original assumption. If $pq = 25$, then $(p, q) = (25, 1), (5, 5), (1, 25)$. None of the three pairs satisfies $p - q = 10$. If $pq = 75$, then $(p, q) = (75, 1), (25, 3), (15, 5), \cdots$. As one can see, $p - q = 10$ is satisfied if $(p, q) = (15, 5)$. Therefore, the sum of digits of p and q must be $1 + 5 + 5 = 11$. The answer is (D).

22. (C)

$\gcd((x+27)(x+37), x) = \gcd(x, 999)$. Since $999 = 27 \cdot 37$. Consider $x = 27k$ for $k = 1, 2, 3$. The reason why $k \geq 4$ does not work is because x must be a two-digit integer. Then, $\gcd(27k, 999) = 27$ for $k = 1, 2, 3$. Consider $x = 37k$ for $k = 1, 2$. Similar to the previous case, this case only allows two values of k since $x \leq 99$. Then, $\gcd(37k, 999) = 37$. Since 37 is greater than 27, the answer is (C).

23. (D)

$\gcd(f(201), f(200)) = \gcd(f(200), 201^2 - 201 + 2020 - 200^2 + 201 - 2020)$, according to Euclidean Algorithm. Since $f(200) = 200^2 - 200 + 2020 = 41820$, and $201^2 - 201 + 2020 - 200^2 + 200 - 2020 = 400$, we are looking for the greatest common divisor of 41820 and 400. Apply Euclidean Algorithm to get $\gcd(41820, 400) = \gcd(400, 220) = \gcd(220, 180) = \gcd(180, 40) = \gcd(40, 20) = \gcd(20, 0) = 20$. Hence, the answer is (D).

24. (B)

Compute $g = \gcd(2^{2015} - 1, 2^{1001} - 1) = \gcd(2^{1001} - 1, 2^{13} - 1)$. Notice that if $x = 2^{13}$, then $2^{1001} = (2^{13})^{77} = x^{77}$, and $x^{77} - 1 = (x - 1)(x^{76} + x^{75} + \cdots + 1)$. Hence, $g = 2^{13} - 1 = 8191$. Find all primes $p \leq \sqrt{8191}$, so $p = 2, 3, 5, 7, 11, 13, 17, 19, \cdots, 89$. Manually check that none of the primes divides 8191. Hence, $g = 8191^1 = p_1^{a_1}$. Hence, $\sum_{i=1}^{k} S(p_i) = S(p_1) = 8 + 1 + 9 + 1 = 19$. The answer is (B).

25. (C)

In this question, we would like to see how 1156324 is a multiple of 37. Notice that $1156324 = 1 \cdot 10^6 + 156 \cdot 10^3 + 324 = 1 \cdot (10^6 - 1) + 156 \cdot (10^3 - 1) + (1 + 156 + 324)$. Since $10^3 - 1 = 999 = 27 \cdot 37$, we use this fact to write $1156324 = 999k + (1 + 156 + 324)$ for some large integer k. Since $999k + 481 = 37(27k + 13)$, we conclude that 1156324 is a multiple of 37. Hence, the answer is (C).

26. (D)

$\gcd(23n+13, 7n-4) = \gcd(7n-4, 2n+25) = \gcd(2n+25, n-79) = \gcd(n-79, 183)$.
Since $n > 79$ and $n \in \mathbb{Z}$, notice that $\gcd(n-79, 183)$ can be either 1, 3, 61, and 183. The sum of these four values is $1+3+61+183 = 248$. The answer is (D).

27. (C)

This is a famous Bezout's identity. $1001a + 3927b$ is a multiple of the greatest common divisor of 1001 and 3927. Notice that
$\gcd(3927, 1001) = \gcd(1001, 924) = \gcd(924, 77) = \gcd(77, 0) = 77$. Hence, $1001a + 3927b = 77k$ for some k. The smallest possible whole number must be 77. The sum of digits of 77 is 14. The answer is (C).

28. (D)

Apply Euclidean Algorithm. $\gcd(2^{297}-1, 2^{288}-1) = \gcd(2^{288}-1, 2^9-1)$. Let $x = 2^9$. Then, $2^{288} = x^{32}$. Hence, $\gcd(x^{32}-1, x-1) = x-1 = 2^9-1 = 511$. The answer is (D).

29. (A)

Let $n = 475a + 100b + 15c + d$. Then, $2n = 950a + 200b + 30c + 2d$. Hence, $1096 - 2n = 200a + 120b$. Use Bezout's identity to conclude that $200a + 120b$ is a multiple of 40. Hence, $1096 - 2n = 40k$ for some integer k. Therefore, $1096 - 2n \equiv 0 \pmod{40}$. Thus, $1096 \equiv 16 \equiv 2n \pmod{40}$. This implies that $n \equiv 8 \pmod{20}$. Thus, $n = 8, 28, 48, \cdots$ or $n = -12, -32, -52, \cdots$. Since $|n| = 8, 12, 28, 32, \cdots$, the smallest possible value of $|n|$ is 8. The answer is (A).

30. (E)

First, if we have time constraints, we would dive for direct computation. In other words, the fourth-power sum equals

$$25333 = 2303 \times 11$$
$$= 7 \times 11 \times 329$$
$$= 7^2 \times 11 \times 47$$

Bezout's identity implies that $|7^2 \times 11 \times 47 \times n - 7 \times 11 \times 13 \times m|$ is a multiple of 77. The smallest integer must be 77. This is the quickest way of solving this question. That being written, the following method shows a general way of producing a formula to compute $\sum_{i=1}^{10} i^4$. In fact, $1^4 + 2^4 + 3^4 + \cdots + 10^4$ is equal to the number of 5-tuples $(a_1, a_2, a_3, a_4, a_5)$ where $a_5 > a_i$ for $i = 1, 2, 3, 4$, and a_i's are elements of $\{1, 2, 3, 4, \cdots, 11\}$. To be specific, if $a_5 = 2$, then there is 1 choice for a_i's respectively to get 1^4. If $a_5 = 3$, then there are 2 choices for a_i's respectively to get 2^4. If $a_5 = 4$, then there are 3 choices for a_i's respectively to get 3^4. You should understand this as an application of permutation allowing repetition. Now, how do we find the number of 5-tuples? We simply perform casework.

First, if there are 2 distinct numbers used in the 5-tuples, there are $\binom{11}{2}$ ways of choosing two numbers and 1 way of arranging the two numbers. For instance, if $\{1, 5\}$ are chosen, then $(1, 1, 1, 1, 5)$ is the only tuple we get. Second, if there are 3 distinct numbers used in the 5-tuples, there are $\binom{11}{3}$ ways of choosing three numbers and there are 14 ways of arranging the three numbers. For instance, if $\{1, 2, 5\}$ are chosen, then $(1, 1, 1, 2, 5)$, $(1, 1, 2, 2, 5)$ and $(1, 2, 2, 2, 5)$ generate $4 + 6 + 4 = 14$ number of ways of arranging the respective tuples, while fixing the last a_5 position. Third, if there are 4 distinct numbers used in the 5-tuples, there are $\binom{11}{4}$ ways of choosing four numbers, and there are 36 ways of arranging the four numbers. For instance, if $\{1, 2, 3, 5\}$ are chosen, then $(1, 2, 3, 3, 5)$, $(1, 2, 2, 3, 5)$ and $(1, 1, 2, 3, 5)$ generate $36 (= 3 \times \binom{4!}{2})$ ways of arranging the respective tuples. Lastly, if there are 5 distinct numbers used in the 5-tuples, there are $\binom{11}{5}$ ways of choosing five numbers, and there are $4!$ ways of arranging the first four numbers, while fixing a_5 as the biggest element. Hence, we get

$$\binom{11}{2} \times 1 + \binom{11}{3} \times 14 + \binom{11}{4} \times 36 + \binom{11}{5} \times 24 = 25333$$

which corresponds to the sum of fourth powers from 1 to 10. Now, if we prime factorize 25333 into $11 \times 7^2 \times 47$. Then, we use Bezout's identity to come up with the same answer (E).

2.4 Application of LCM and GCD

When we deal with integers, it is common to find some questions in competition math applying the knowledge of least common multiples or greatest common divisors. This requires some thoughts, and in most of the times, it can be resolved using some caseworks and properly labeling the given pieces of information. Let's have a look at the following example.

Example If $\text{lcm}(24, t) = 40 \gcd(24, t)$, find the possible values of t.

Step-by-Step Solution

#1. Let $t = 2^a 3^b k$ where k involves some other primes than 2 or 3.
#2. $\text{lcm}(2^3 3^1, 2^a 3^b k) = 40 \cdot \gcd(2^3 3^1, 2^a 3^b k) \implies 2^{\max(3,a)} 3^{\max(1,b)} k = 40 \cdot 2^{\min(3,a)} 3^{\min(1,b)}$.
#3. Notice that $40 = 2^3 \cdot 5$. Use this to rewrite the equation above.
#4. $2^{\max(3,a)} 3^{\max(1,b)} k = 2^{3+\min(3,a)} 3^{\min(1,b)} 5^1$.
#5. Let's just have a look at powers of 2. $\max(3, a) = 3 + \min(3, a)$ can be written as $3 = 3 + 3$, $3 = 3 + a$, $a = 3 + 3$, or $a = 3 + a$. Here, $a = 0$ or 6.
#6. Likewise, have a look at powers of 3. $\max(1, b) = \min(1, b)$ implies that $1 = 1$, $b = b$, $1 = b$ or $b = 1$. In any case, even after eliminating some impossible conclusions, we get $b = 1$.
#7. $k = 5$, which seems obvious.
#8. Therefore, $t = 2^0 3^1 5$ or $2^3 3^1 5$. Hence, $t = 15$ or 120.

We should be careful when we perform caseworks, but since there are four possibilities to think of, you should write down all possibilities, then check with the original assumption to test whether the given values are valid.

Basic Drill 7

1. If the sum of two positive integers m and n equals 2020, find the largest possible value of $\gcd(m, n)$.

2. The greatest common divisor of positive integers m and n is 4. The least common multiple of m and n is 60. Compute the least possible value of $m + n$.

3. Find the number of all positive integers n for which $\mathrm{lcm}[n, 10] = 30$.

4. If the least common multiple of n and m is 595, and the ratio of n to m is $5 : 7$, then find the greatest common divisor of n and m.

Answer to Basic Drill 7

1.

If $m = n = 1010$, then $m + n = 2020$ and $\gcd(m, n) = (1010, 1010) = 1010$. If $m > n$ or $m < n$, then the smaller value is always less than 1010, so $\gcd(m, n)$ is always less than 1010. Therefore, the largest possible value of $\gcd(m, n) = \boxed{1010}$.

2.

Notice that $m = 4x$ and $n = 4y$ for some relatively prime x and y. The original condition states that $4xy = 60$, where $xy = 15$. Since $m + n = 4(x + y)$ is to be minimized, $(x, y) = (1, 15), (3, 5), (5, 3)$ and $(15, 1)$ imply that $m + n$ is minimized when $(x, y) = (3, 5)$ or $(5, 3)$. Thus, the minimum value of $m + n$ is $\boxed{32}$.

3.

First, 10 is not divisible by 3, but 30 is divisible by 3. Let $n = 3m$ for some m. Then, $\text{lcm}[3m, 2 \cdot 5] = 2 \cdot 3 \cdot 5$ implies $m = 1, 2, 5, 10$. Hence, there are $\boxed{4}$ values of m.

4.

Let $n = 5x$ and $m = 7x$ for some x. Since 5 and 7 are relatively prime, x must be the greatest common divisor of n and m. Hence, $(5)(7)x = 35x = 595$ implies that $x = 17$. Therefore, $\boxed{17}$ is the greatest common divisor.

Practice

31. Suppose t is a positive integer such that $(\text{lcm}[18, t])^3 = (18t)^2$. What is the sum of all possible values for t?

(A) 12
(B) 324
(C) 336
(D) 348
(E) 660

32. Given a positive integer n, $\text{lcm}[125n, 10^{10}] = 25 \cdot \text{lcm}[n, 10^{10}]$, then $n = 5^\alpha K$ for some integer K and α, where $K \not\equiv 0 \pmod 5$. Which of the following is the sum of all possible values of α?

(A) 8
(B) 9
(C) 15
(D) 17
(E) 19

33. Suppose that a is a positive integer for which the least common multiple of $2a + 2$ and $2a - 4$ is 27140. Find the number of distinct digits of $a^2 - a$.
(A) 4
(B) 5
(C) 6
(D) 7
(E) 8

34. When the greatest common divisor and least common multiple of two integers are multiplied, the product is 240. How many different values could be the greatest common divisor of the two integers?
(A) 1
(B) 2
(C) 3
(D) 4
(E) 5

35. Suppose p and q are positive integers such that $\gcd(p, q)$ is divisible by exactly 47 distinct primes and $\text{lcm}[p, q]$ is divisible by exactly 2020 distinct primes. If q has more distinct prime factors than p, then q has at least how many distinct prime factors?

(A) 986

(B) 987

(C) 1033

(D) 1034

(E) 2020

36. There are $9,000$ number of 8-digit integers formed by repeating a positive four-digit integer. For example, $12,341,234$ or $98,719,871$ are integers of this form. What is the largest prime factor of the greatest common divisor of all eight-digit integers of this form?

(A) 31

(B) 71

(C) 113

(D) 137

(E) 171

37. The greatest common divisor of two 2-digit positive integers is equal to 3. Their least common multiple is six times the greatest of the two integers. What is the largest possible sum of the two integers?

(A) 99
(B) 102
(C) 105
(D) 108
(E) 111

38. If m and n are positive integers such that $\gcd(m, n) = 30030$, $\text{lcm}[m, n] = (30030)^3$, and $m < n$, how many distinct pairs of (m, n) are there?

(A) 8
(B) 16
(C) 32
(D) 64
(E) 128

39. If the product of the greatest common divisor and the least common multiple of two positive integers is equal to 180, find the number of distinct ordered pairs of the two integers.
(A) 16
(B) 18
(C) 20
(D) 22
(E) 24

40. How many integers n are there such that $0 < n \leq 100$ and $\gcd(n, 100)$ is a two-digit number?
(A) 10
(B) 11
(C) 12
(D) 13
(E) 14

Answer Key from 31 to 40

31. (C)

First, $18t = \text{lcm}(18, t)\gcd(18, t)$. Hence, $\text{lcm}(18, t) = \gcd(18, t)^2$. Hence, $2^{\max(1,a)}3^{\max(2,b)}K = 2^{2\min(1,a)}3^{2\min(1,b)}$ where $t = 2^a 3^b K$ where K consists of other primes than 2 or 3. Then, $a = 2$ without any exception. Nevertheless, $b = 1$ or 4, depending on whether $b < 2$ or $b > 2$. Also, there is no other prime other than 2 or 3, so $K = 1$. Thus, $t = 2^2 3^1$ or $t = 2^2 3^4$. The sum of these two values is 336.

32. (B)

Since we are looking for possible values of α, stick to the powers of 5. The left-hand side of the expression has its powers of 5 as $5^{\max(\alpha+3,10)}$, and the right-hand side of the expression has its powers of 5 as $5^{2+\max(\alpha,10)}$. We are solving for $\max(\alpha + 3, 10) = 2 + \max(\alpha, 10)$. Let's have a look at all possible cases. First, assume that $\alpha + 3 > 10$ and $\alpha > 10$. Then, $\alpha + 3 = 2 + \alpha$, which is false. Second, assume that $\alpha + 3 > 10$ and $\alpha < 10$. Then, $\alpha + 3 = 2 + 10$, so $\alpha = 9$. Third, assume that $10 > \alpha + 3$ and $10 > \alpha$. Then, $10 = 2 + 10$, which is false. Hence, there is only one possible value of α. The answer is (B).

33. (B)

First, let's compute the greatest common divisor between $2a + 2$ and $2a - 4$. Apply Euclidean Algorithm to find out that $\gcd(2a + 2, 2a - 4) = \gcd(2a - 4, 6)$. This implies that the greatest common divisor must be one of the factors of 6. Since the least common multiple is a multiple of the greatest common divisor, and 27140 is not a multiple of 3, so we conclude that $\gcd(2a + 2, 2a - 4) = 2$. Hence, $(2a + 2)(2a - 4) = 2^2(a + 1)(a - 2) = 2 \cdot 27140$. Hence, $a^2 - a - 2 = 13570$. Therefore, $a^2 - a = 13572$. There are 5 distinct digits in 13572, so the answer is (B).

34. (C)

Let $a = gx$ and $b = gy$ for the original two integers, where g is the greatest common divisor of a and b and x and y are relatively prime. Then, $ab = 240 = g^2 xy$. Now, prime factorize 240 into $2^4 \cdot 3 \cdot 5$. Since g^2 is a perfect square, we conclude that $g^2 \in \{2^0, 2^2, 2^4\}$. Hence, there are three possible values for g. The answer is (C).

35. (D)

Let $g = \gcd(p, q)$ and $p = gx$ and $q = gy$ for some relatively prime x and y. Since the least common multiple of p and q can be written as gxy, xy must consist of 1973 distinct primes. Since q has more distinct prime factors than q, at least we must set $(p, q) = (n, n + 1)$ in order to find the smallest possible value for q. Hence, $2n + 1 = 1973$ indicates that y contains at least 987 distinct primes. Hence, q contains 1034 number of distinct primes. The answer is (D).

76 The Essential Guide to **Competition Math** [Number Theory]

36. (D)

Notice that all 8-digit integers in this form has the common factor of 10001. Prime factorize it into $73 \cdot 137$, so the answer is (D).

37. (E)

Let a and b be these two 2-digit positive integers. Without loss of generality, assume $a \geq b$. Also, assume that $a = 3x$ and $b = 3y$ where x and y are relatively prime. Then, $3xy = 6(3x)$, so $y = 6$. Notice that $b = 18$. We start investigating the value of a from $a = 99, 96, 93, 90, \cdots$. If $a = 99, 96$, then it contradicts the original assumption that the greatest common divisor is 3. Hence, the largest possible value of a must be 93. Therefore, the sum of a and b is $93 + 18 = 111$. The answer is (E).

38. (C)

Let $m = gx$ and $n = gy$ for g the greatest common divisor, and x and y relatively prime integers. Then, $xy = (30030)^2$. Since $xy = (2 \cdot 3 \cdot 5 \cdot 7 \cdot 11 \cdot 13)^2$. There are 2^6 distinct pairs for (x, y). Since $x < y$ and x and y can't share prime factors, we get $32 = 2^6/2$ number of pairs for (x, y). Thus, there are 32 pairs of $(m, n) = (gx, gy)$. The answer is (C).

39. (B)

We need to perform caseworks on g. First, $g^2 xy = 180 = 2^2 \cdot 3^2 \cdot 5$. If $g^2 = 1$, then $xy = 2^2 \cdot 3^2 \cdot 5$, so there are $2^3 = 8$ distinct pairs of (x, y). If $g^2 = 2^2$, then $xy = 3^2 \cdot 5$, so there are $2^2 = 4$ distinct pairs of (x, y). If $g^2 = 3^2$, then $xy = 2^2 \cdot 5$, so there are $2^2 = 4$ distinct pairs of (x, y). If $g^2 = 6^2$, then $xy = 5$, so there are 2 pairs of (x, y). In total, there are 18 distinct pairs of (gx, gy). The answer is (B).

40. (B)

It is easy to check that if n is a multiple of 10, then $\gcd(n, 100) \geq 10$. Hence, $n = 10, 20, 30, \cdots, 90$. On the other hand, if n is a multiple of 25, then $\gcd(n, 100) \geq 25$. Hence, $n = 25, 75$. (We skip $n = 50$ since it has been already counted in the earlier case.) Hence, there are 11 possible values of n such that the greatest common divisor of n and 100 is a 2-digit integer.

Did you know?

1. Thanks to Number Theory, public key encryptography allows online transactions, using primes and composites.

2. Sending direct messages to your friend via Instagram also uses Number Theory.

3. Alan Turing, the most important figure in the history of computer science, cracked German naval code, known as Enigma, by using Number Theory.

4. In world war 2, US experts decoded Japanese naval codes by using Number Theory, basically using modular arithmetic and multiplicative inverses.

5. Cryptocurrency, famous for Bitcoin, also uses Number Theory as its foundation.

6. Quasi-random number gerenation, which uses Number Theory, is widely used in financial engineering, especially when determining the price of financial derivatives or producing different portfolio scenarios.

7. In virology, Number Theory is used to figure out the structure of viruses, solving Diophantine equations for geometric symmetries.

8. Quantum physics also uses Number Theory, not to mention Hardy-Ramanujan formula that approximates the number of partition of a given natural number n.

9. Number Theory is also used in the theory of sequences over finite fields, which is applied in the testing of Einstein's law of relativity.

TOPIC 3

Counting Divisors and More Arithmetic

3.1 Counting Divisors and More Arithmetic

Counting divisors utilizes the principle of multiplication. For instance, if $n = p_1^{q_1} p_2^{q_2} \cdots p_k^{q_k}$, where $k \geq 1$ and $q_i \geq 0$ for $i = 1, 2, \cdots, k$, then the number of divisors can be found by using the following principle.

#1. For p_1's, we can select one out of $\{p_1^0, p_1^1, \cdots, p_1^{q_1}\}$. In other words, there are $q_1 + 1$ number of possible choices to make for p_1.

#2. For p_2's, we can select one out of $\{p_2^0, p_2^1, \cdots, p_2^{q_2}\}$. In other words, there are $q_2 + 1$ number of possible choices to make for p_2.

$$\vdots$$

#k. For p_k's, we can select one out of $\{p_k^0, p_k^1, \cdots, p_k^{q_k}\}$. In other words, there are $q_k + 1$ number of possible choices to make for p_k.

Therefore, there are

$$(1 + q_1)(1 + q_2) \cdots (1 + q_k)$$

number of positive divisors of n.

There are two additional arithmetics related to counting divisors. The first is the sum of divisors.

Example Find the sum of positive divisors of 12.

Step-by-step Solution

#1. First, $12 = 2^2 \cdot 3$.

#2. Notice that $1 + 2 + 3 + 4 + 6 + 12 = (1 + 3) + (2 + 6) + (4 + 12) = (1 + 3)(1 + 2 + 4)$.

#3. In particular, $(1 + 3)(1 + 2 + 4) = (3^0 + 3^1)(2^0 + 2^1 + 2^2)$. Now, 2^2 produces $\{1, 2, 2^2\}$ and 3^1 produces $\{1, 3^1\}$ possible factors of 12. Since we are taking the sum of divisors, we need to count each divisor once, so $(1 + 2 + 2^2)(1 + 3^1)$ does the trick.

The second application is the product of divisors.

Example Find the product of positive divisors of 12.

Step-by-step Solution

#1. Write down all positive divisors of 12, i.e., $\{1, 2, 3, 4, 6, 12\}$.

#2. Pair up divisors of 12 as $(1, 12), (2, 6), (3, 4)$.

#3. The product of all divisors are, in fact, powers of 12, where the exponent is half the number of divisors.

Basic Drill 8

1. Find the sum of positive divisors of 100.

2. Find the sum of even positive divisors of 84.

3. Find the product of all positive odd divisors of 18.

4. Find the number of perfect square divisors of $2^4 \cdot 3^4 \cdot 5^4$.

Answer to Basic Drill 8

1.

First, prime factorize 100 into $100 = 2^2 \cdot 5^2$. Then, the sum of divisors can be found by case enumeration on the number of 2's in the divisors. If there is no 2, then the only divisors we take in are 1, 5, and 25. Similarly, if there is one 2, then the only divisors we have are $2 \cdot 1$, $2 \cdot 5$ and $2 \cdot 25$. Likewise, if there are two 2s, then the divisors we have are 2^2, $2^2 \cdot 5$ and $2^2 \cdot 25$. Hence, the total sum of these divisors can be found by the following expression, i.e., $(1 + 2 + 2^2)(1 + 5 + 5^2) = (7)(31) = \boxed{217}$.

2.

First, prime factorize 84 into $84 = 2^2 \cdot 3 \cdot 7$. We take a similar approach as we did in question 1, except that we must take at least one 2. That being said, if the total sum of all positive divisors must have been $(1 + 2 + 2^2)(1 + 3)(1 + 7)$, but the ones for which are accounted must be $2(1 + 3 + 7 + 21)$ and $2^2(1 + 3 + 7 + 21)$. Hence, the sum of positive even divisors is $(2 + 2^2)(1 + 3)(1 + 7) = \boxed{192}$.

3.

First, prime factorize 18 into $18 = 2 \cdot 3^2$. All factors of 18 must be written as $2^a 3^b$ where $0 \leq a \leq 1$ and $0 \leq b \leq 2$. Since all odd divisors have no 2 in their factorization, we let $a = 0$. On the other hand, there is no restriction in b's, so we let $b = 0, 1,$ and 2. Therefore, the product of all positive odd divisors equals $1 \cdot 3 \cdot 9 = \boxed{27}$.

4.

First, 2^4 has 1, 2^2 and 2^4 as its perfect square divisors. Second, 3^4 has 1, 3^2 and 3^4 as its perfect square divisors. Third, 5^4 has 1, 5^2 and 5^4 as its perfect square divisors. Thus, in total, there are $\boxed{27}$ number of perfect square divisors of the original number.

Practice

1. Bob plays with his square unit tiles by arranging all of them into different shaped rectangular figures. He can make a 2 by 3 rectangle by using 6 tiles and considers it equal to a 3 by 2 rectangle. Bob can form exactly eighteen different rectangular figures that each uses all of his tiles. What is the least number of tiles Bob could have?

(A) 1024

(B) 1208

(C) 1260

(D) 1440

(E) 1690

2. How many even perfect square factors does $2^{12} \cdot 3^9 \cdot 7^5$ have?

(A) 60

(B) 90

(C) 120

(D) 150

(E) 180

3. Find the number of "integer" pairs (a, b) satisfying $\frac{1}{a} + \frac{1}{b} = \frac{1}{12}$.

(A) 28
(B) 29
(C) 30
(D) 31
(E) 32

4. If $n = 2^5 \cdot 3^6 \cdot 5^7$, how many of the natural-number factors of n are multiples of 120?

(A) 100
(B) 121
(C) 126
(D) 144
(E) 154

5. Bo places 800 marbles into m total boxes such that each box contains an equal number of marbles, let's say n marbles. If there is unlimited number of boxes, where each box contains more than one marble, and he wants to place the marbles into more than one box, for how many values of m can this be done?
(A) 16
(B) 17
(C) 18
(D) 19
(E) 20

6. How many ordered pairs (x, y) of positive integers satisfy the equation $xy = 900$ and $x < y$?
(A) 12
(B) 13
(C) 24
(D) 26
(E) 27

7. Two positive integers a and b are chosen such that a is the smallest odd positive 2-digit integer with only even number of positive divisors and b is the largest integer less than $1,000$ with exactly three positive divisors. What is $a + b$?

(A) 964

(B) 967

(C) 970

(D) 972

(E) 974

8. Find the sum of all integer ks that will make the expression $\dfrac{19}{k-61} + \dfrac{20}{k-61} + \dfrac{21}{k-61}$ an integer value.

(A) 0

(B) 1024

(C) 1464

(D) 1892

(E) 2025

9. For positive integer n such that $n < 1000$, the number "$n + 100$" has exactly 8 positive factors. Find the smallest possible value of n.

(A) 1
(B) 2
(C) 3
(D) 4
(E) 5

10. What is the sum of the positive two-digit factors of 48?

(A) 84
(B) 88
(C) 92
(D) 96
(E) 100

11. The sum of the positive divisors of a positive integer of the form $2^i 3^j$ is equal to 600. What is $i + j$?

(A) 3
(B) 4
(C) 5
(D) 6
(E) 7

12. If the product of the positive integer divisors of 100 equals 10^p where p is an integer, find the value of $s(p)$ where $s(n)$ is the sum of digits of n.

(A) 3
(B) 6
(C) 9
(D) 12
(E) 15

13. It is well-known that $1 + r + r^2 + r^3 + \cdots = \frac{1}{1-r}$ where $0 < |r| < 1$. For example, $1 + \frac{1}{2} + \frac{1}{4} + \frac{1}{8} + \cdots = \frac{1}{1-1/2} = 2$. Find the sum of all reciprocals of natural numbers greater than 1, whose prime factorization consists of only 3 or 5.

(A) $\frac{2}{3}$
(B) $\frac{4}{5}$
(C) $\frac{3}{4}$
(D) $\frac{7}{8}$
(E) $\frac{7}{9}$

14. The product of the positive integer divisors of a positive integer n is 32768. How many positive divisors of n are there?

(A) 3
(B) 4
(C) 5
(D) 6
(E) 7

15. If A is the sum of the positive divisors of 500, what is the sum of the distinct prime divisors of A?

(A) 17
(B) 18
(C) 20
(D) 22
(E) 25

16. Out of odd positive divisors of 630, there are eight multiples of 3. Find the sum of these multiples of 3.

(A) 288
(B) 369
(C) 576
(D) 729
(E) 961

17. Find the sum of positive divisors of the smallest positive integer with exactly 12 positive distinct divisors.

(A) 121
(B) 145
(C) 168
(D) 196
(E) 216

18. What is the sum of all of odd positive divisors of 540, where each of the divisors is a multiple of 15?

(A) 155
(B) 175
(C) 195
(D) 215
(E) 235

19. For how many integers n between -1000 and -1, inclusive, is the product of both negative and positive divisors (including all improper divisors) of n negative?

(A) 29
(B) 30
(C) 31
(D) 32
(E) 33

20. What is the smallest positive integer n whose positive divisors have a product of n^8?

(A) 90
(B) 150
(C) 210
(D) 270
(E) 330

Answer Key from 1 to 20

1. (C)

There are 36 positive divisors. Let's categorize 36 into the following sub-cases.

$$36 = 36$$
$$= 18 \times 2$$
$$= 9 \times 4$$
$$= 6 \times 6$$
$$= 9 \times 2 \times 2$$
$$= 6 \times 3 \times 2$$
$$= 3 \times 3 \times 2 \times 2$$

If there is one prime factor, then the least number is 2^{35}. If there are two prime factors, then the least number $2^5 \cdot 3^5$. If there are three prime factors, then the least number is $2^5 \cdot 3^2 \cdot 5$. If there are four prime factors, then the least number is $2^2 \cdot 3^2 \cdot 5 \cdot 7 = 1260$. The answer is (C).

2. (B)

First, one of the powers of 2 from $\{2^2, 2^4, \cdots, 2^{12}\}$ can be selected. Second, one of the powers of 3 from $\{3^0, 3^2, 3^4, 3^6, 3^8\}$ can be selected. Third, one of the powers of 7 from $\{7^0, 7^2, 7^4\}$ can be selected. Hence, there are 90 even perfect squares.

3. (B)

The original equation turns into $ab = 12a + 12b$. Hence, by Simon's Favorite Factoring Technique, it turns into $ab - 12a - 12b = 144$. Hence, $(a - 12)(b - 12) = 144$. Since $144 = 2^4 \cdot 3^2$, there are 5×3 positive pairs of (a, b). Likewise, there are 5×3 negative pairs of (a, b). Hence, there should be 30 pairs of (a, b). However, $(a, b) = (0, 0)$ must be excluded from the list, since $a, b \neq 0$. Therefore, there are 29 pairs of (a, b).

4. (C)

A multiple of 120 has at least 2^3, 3^1 or 5^1. Hence, for powers of 2, there are 3 possible choices for natural factors of n. For powers of 3, there are 6 possible choices. For powers of 7, there are 7 possible choices. Hence, there are 126 factors of n that are multiples of 120.

5. (A)

Since $800 = mn$ where $800 = 2^5 5^2$, there are 18 possible pairs of (m, n). Since $m \neq 1$ or $n \neq 1$, we eliminate $(m, n) = (800, 1)$ and $(m, n) = (1, 800)$. Hence, there are 15 pairs of (m, n).

6. (B)

The number of (x, y) pairs satisfying $xy = 900$ equals the number of divisors of 900. Since $900 = 2^2 3^2 5^2$, there are 27 pairs of (x, y) satisfying $xy = 900$. Since $x < y$, we must get rid of $(x, y) = (30, 30)$, and divide the remaining 26 pairs into half, due to symmetry between $x < y$ and $x > y$. Therefore, there are 13 pairs of (x, y).

7. (D)

Notice that a positive integer with two divisors is prime. Hence, $a = 11$. Likewise, a positive integer with three divisors is the perfect square of a prime number. Hence, $b = 961 = 31^2$. Therefore, $a + b = 972$.

8. (C)

Since $\frac{60}{k-61}$ is an integer, $k - 61$ must be a divisor of 60, either positive or negative. Hence, $k - 61 = \pm 1, \pm 2, \pm 3, \cdots, \pm 60$. Since there are 24 values of $k - 61$, which offset by pairs, the sum of all values k will be $61 \times 24 = 1464$.

9. (B)

First, $101 \leq n + 100 < 10,100$. There could be one prime, two primes or three primes. If there is one prime, $n + 100 = p^7$. If there are two primes, $n + 100 = p^3 q$. If there are three primes, $n + 100 = pqr$, where p, q, and r are primes. By testing some small primes, $n + 100 = 2 \cdot 3 \cdot 17 = 102$ is the smallest possible value of $n + 100$. Therefore, the answer is (B).

10. (E)

Since $48 = 2^4 \cdot 3$, the sum of all divisors is $(1 + 2 + 2^2 + 2^3 + 2^4)(1 + 3) = 124$. Get rid of a single-digit divisor, i.e., $\{1, 2, 3, 4, 6, 8\}$, so the sum of two-digit divisors of 48 equals 100.

11. (D)

First, set up $(1 + 2 + \cdots + 2^i)(1 + 3 + \cdots + 3^j) = 600$. If there are exponential expressions involving integer exponent, we always perform casework. If $j = 1$, then $1 + 2 + \cdots + 2^i = 2^{i+1} - 1 = 150$. There is no such i. If $j = 2$, then $2^{i+1} - 1 = 600/13$. There is no such i as well. If $j = 3$, then $2^{i+1} - 1 = 15$, and $i = 3$. Hence, $i + j = 3 + 3 = 6$. The answer is (D).

12. (C)

Check that $\{1, 2, 4, 5, 10, 20, 25, 50, 100\}$ has its pair $(1, 100), (2, 50), (4, 25), (5, 20)$, and 10, so that there are $9/2$ number of pairs, where 9 represents the number of positive divisors of 100. Hence, the product of positive divisors of 100 equals $100^{9/2} = 10^9$. Since $p = 9$, $s(9) = 9$. Therefore, the answer is (C).

13. (D)

Imagine having 1 in the expression. Then, it turns out to be a product of two infinite series involving $1/3$ and $1/5$.

$$1 + \frac{1}{3} + \frac{1}{5} + \frac{1}{9} + \frac{1}{15} + \cdots = \left(1 + \frac{1}{3} + \frac{1}{9} + \cdots\right)\left(1 + \frac{1}{5} + \frac{1}{25} + \cdots\right)$$
$$= \frac{1}{1 - 1/3} \times \frac{1}{1 - 1/5} = \frac{15}{8}$$

Since 1 is excluded, subtract 1 from the sum to get $\frac{7}{8}$.

14. (D)

Notice that $32768 = 2^{15}$. Since $2^{0+1+2+3+4+5} = 2^{15}$, 32768 must be the product of positive divisors of $2^5 = 32$. Hence, there are 6 divisors of 32. The answer is (D).

15. (E)

First, $500 = 2^2 5^3$. Therefore, the sum of divisors of 500 is $(1 + 2 + 4)(1 + 5 + 25 + 125) = 7 \cdot 156$, which can be factorized into $2^2 \cdot 3 \cdot 7 \cdot 13$. Hence, the sum of distinct prime divisors of A is 25. The answer is (E).

16. (C)

Notice that $630 = 2 \cdot 3^2 \cdot 5 \cdot 7$. The sum of multiples of 3, which are divisors of 630 at the same time, can be written as $(3 + 3^2)(1 + 5)(1 + 7) = 576$. The answer is (C).

17. (C)

The smallest positive integer with exactly 12 positive distinct divisors is $2^2 3^1 5^1 = 60$. Hence, the sum of positive divisors of 60 can be found as $(1 + 2 + 2^2)(1 + 3)(1 + 5) = 168$. The answer is (C).

18. (C)

Out of divisors of 540, odd divisors of 540 can be found as divisors of $3^3 \cdot 5$. Since we are looking for multiples of 15, we can write them as $3 \cdot 5$, $3^2 \cdot 5$ and $3^3 \cdot 5$. Hence, the sum of these three numbers is 195. The answer is (C).

19. (C)

Notice that a perfect square has odd number of divisors. At the same time, if there is -1 in front of a perfect square, we can easily check that the product of both negative and positive divisors will still be negative. For instance, $-1 \cdot 1 < 0$, $-1 \cdot 1 \cdot -2 \cdot 2 \cdot -4 \cdot 4 < 0$, and so on. Note that if the question allows proper divisors, then the given range must have been different. However, if we look a perfect squares, then there are odd number of divisors, so -1 appears also odd number of times. Since there are 31 negative perfect squares between -1000 and -1, inclusive, the answer is (C).

20. (C)

Given a positive integer N, assume that its prime factorization is given by

$$N = p_1^{q_1} p_2^{q_2} \cdots p_n^{q_n}$$

Then, the product of its divisors is given by $N^{\frac{\prod_{i=1}^{n}(q_i+1)}{2}}$. Since there are 16 divisors, we make it into four prime scenario such that $16 = 2 \cdot 2 \cdot 2 \cdot 2$. The smallest possible number must be the product of 2, 3, 5, and 7, so it must be 210. The answer is (C).

TOPIC 4

Base-N Expression

4.1 Base-N Expression

A counting number that we normally uses follows base-10. In fact, if there is a natural number n, we can write it as $n = \overline{A_k A_{k-1} A_{k-2} \cdots A_0}_{(10)}$, where

$$n = A_k \cdot 10^k + A_{k-1} \cdot 10^{k-1} + A_{k-2} \cdot 10^{k-2} + \cdots + A_0 \cdot 10^0$$

such that A_i's are between 0 and 9, inclusive.

If we generalize this result, we can use different bases, i.e., base-N. If we count a number using base-N, then we start counting it by

$$1, 2, 3, \cdots, N-1, N, N+1, \cdots$$

where $N = 1 \cdot N^1 + 0 \cdot N^0 = \overline{10}_N$, $N+1 = 1 \cdot N^1 + 1 \cdot N^0 = \overline{11}_N$, and so on. One important fact that we use is that there are N number of digits in base-N, including 0. For instance, if we have base-9 numbers, then the only digits that we can use is $\{0, 1, 2, \cdots, 8\}$. Also, if $N > 10$, then digits from 10 to above are written as alphabets. That being written, we need to go over two types of problems involving base-N expressions.

- Converting base-10 into base-N : write down powers of N smaller than the original number and perform long-division multiple times.

- Converting base-N into base-10 : write the original number in sum of powers of N and simplify the result.

Example Turn $\overline{1234}_5$ into base-10 number.

Step-by-step Solution
#1. First, notice that $\overline{1234}_5 = 1 \cdot 5^3 + 2 \cdot 5^2 + 3 \cdot 5 + 4$.
#2. In base-10, the number equals $125 + 50 + 15 + 4 = 194$.

Example Turn 1234 into base-5 number.

Step-by-step Solution
#1. First, compute powers of 5, i.e., $1, 5, 25, 125, 625$, which are smaller than 1234.
#2. $1234 = 1(625) + 4(125) + 4(25) + 1(5) + 4 = \overline{14414}_5$.

Basic Drill 9

1. Convert the following base-5 number $\overline{1234}_5$ into base-8.

2. If the following two-digit expressions satisfy $\overline{3X}_4 = \overline{X4}_9$ for some valid X, find the value of X.

3. Find the remainder when the base-8 number 111222333_8 is divided by 16.

4. When the base-22 number 12345_{22} is divided by the base-10 number 21, find out the remainder.

Answer to Basic Drill 9

1.

First, $1234_5 = 1(5^3) + 2(5^2) + 3(5) + 4 = 194$. Second, $194 = 3(8^2) + 2$, so $\boxed{302_8}$ is the base-8 expression.

2.

$$3X_4 = X4_9$$
$$3(4) + X = 9(X) + 4$$
$$8 = 8X$$
$$1 = X$$

Therefore, $\boxed{X = 1}$.

3.

$$111222333_8 = 64K + 3(8) + 3$$
$$= 16(4K + 1) + 11$$
$$\equiv 11 \pmod{16}$$

Hence, the remainder is $\boxed{11}$ when the given original number is divided by 16.

4.

$$12345_{22} = 1(21+1)^4 + 2(21+1)^3 + 3(21+1)^2 + 4(21+1) + 5$$
$$= 21K + (1 + 2 + 3 + 4 + 5)$$
$$\equiv 15 \pmod{21}$$

Therefore, the remainder is $\boxed{15}$ when the original number is divided by 21.

Practice

1. Bing, a six-fingered alien, communicated to Bo, an astronaut, via transmission tools, and Bing does not know whether Bo uses base-10 system. As Bing transmitted a number "1234," counted by his fingers, Bo, thinking that Bing uses six fingers efficiently, would best translate it into

(A) 300
(B) 310
(C) 320
(D) 330
(E) 340

2. Assume that a two-digit counting number n is selected at random. If the probability that the base-6 representation and the base-7 representation of n are both two-digit numbers can be written as $\dfrac{p}{q}$ where p and q are relatively prime, find $p + q$.

(A) 56
(B) 57
(C) 58
(D) 59
(E) 60

3. How many base-10 integers are exactly 5 digits in their base-3 representation and exactly 4 digits in their base-6 representation?

(A) 25
(B) 26
(C) 27
(D) 28
(E) 29

4. Which of the following is the greatest prime factor of the largest 4-digit base-17 integer?

(A) 11
(B) 17
(C) 29
(D) 31
(E) 37

5. If $n = \overline{abcd}_8$, where a, b, c, and d represents a base-8 digit, how many n-values are there?
(A) 2560
(B) 3072
(C) 3584
(D) 4096
(E) 5120

6. If $\overline{1dd5}_{13}$ is divisible by the base-10 number 12, which of the following is the product of all possible values of d? (Here, $\overline{1dd5}_{13}$ represents a base-13 number whose first digit is 1, whose last digit is 5, and whose middle two digits are both equal to d).
(A) 3
(B) 9
(C) 15
(D) 24
(E) 27

7. For how many positive integers have their expression in base-9 digits equal to the reverse of their expression in base-17 digits?

(A) 12
(B) 13
(C) 14
(D) 15
(E) 16

8. The base-17 representation of a positive integer is $\overline{X8Z9}_{17}$, which is divisible by 18. How many pairs of (X, Z) satisfying the given condition are there?

(A) 12
(B) 13
(C) 14
(D) 15
(E) 16

9. Let n be a positive integer such that

$$n = \overline{ABC}_7 = \overline{CB}_{12}.$$

Find the value of n in base 10.

(A) 57
(B) 59
(C) 61
(D) 63
(E) 65

10. Suppose a and b are positive integers. When a^2 is written in base-b, the result is $\overline{121}_b$. When b^2 is written in base-a, the result is $\overline{51}_a$. What is a?

(A) 7
(B) 8
(C) 9
(D) 10
(E) 11

11. A certain integer has 4 digits when written in base 16. The same integer has d digits when written in base 2. What is the sum of all possible values of d?

(A) 55
(B) 56
(C) 57
(D) 58
(E) 59

12. A "quick" thermometer always skips digit 9. For example, a thermometer changes directly from 88 to 100. If the actual temperature is 139 units, the thermometer reads a certain number. Find the sum of its digits.

(A) 8
(B) 9
(C) 10
(D) 11
(E) 12

13. The first 2021 positive integers are each written in base-15. How many of these base-15 representations are palindromes? (A palindrome is a number that reads the same forward and backward.)

(A) 140

(B) 142

(C) 144

(D) 146

(E) 148

14. Let the sequence of numbers be $1, 7, 8, 49, 50, 56, 57, \cdots$, whose terms consist of non-negative powers of 7 at most once. If the nth term is 399, find the value of n.

(A) 11

(B) 12

(C) 13

(D) 14

(E) 15

15. When the base-17 integer 123456789_{17} is divided by the base-10 number 16, what is the remainder?

(A) 11
(B) 12
(C) 13
(D) 14
(E) 15

16. Find the number of ordered pairs (A, B) of digits for which $\overline{87AB}_{10}$ is divisible by 15.

(A) 5
(B) 6
(C) 7
(D) 8
(E) 9

17. Find the number of base-10 two-digit numbers whose base-4 and base-5 expansions have the same number of digits.

(A) 45
(B) 46
(C) 47
(D) 48
(E) 49

18. If $S(n)$ is the sum of digits of n, which of the following is the value of the following expression, where there are 2021 times of compositions?

$$S(S(S(S(S(S\cdots(S(1234567891011121314151617181920)\cdots))))))$$

(A) 1
(B) 2
(C) 3
(D) 4
(E) 5

19. Find the number of ordered triples (A, B, C) satisfying $9 \times \overline{BC} = \overline{ABC}$ where A, B, and C are valid digits in base-10.
(A) 0
(B) 1
(C) 2
(D) 3
(E) 4

20. Given $\overline{ABCDE}_5$ where $A \neq 0$, how many 5-digit numbers in base-5 are there such that there is at least one digit repeated more than once?
(A) 2400
(B) 2401
(C) 2402
(D) 2403
(E) 2404

Answer Key from 1 to 20

1. (B)
Bing can only use six fingers to count, so he must be using base-6 system. Since $1234_6 = 1 \cdot 6^3 + 2 \cdot 6^2 + 3 \cdot 6 + 4 = 310$, the answer is (B).

2. (C)
Let n be a 2-digit counting number. Then, $10 \leq n \leq 99$ implies that there are 90 possible numbers for n. Base-6 and base-7 conditions imply that $6 \leq n \leq 6^2 - 1$ and $7 \leq n \leq 7^2 - 1$. Hence, $n = 10, 11, 12, \cdots, 35$. Out of 90 numbers, there are 26 possible values satisfying the given condition. Therefore, $\frac{p}{q} = \frac{13}{45}$, so $p + q = 58$.

3. (C)
Notice that $3^4 \leq n \leq 3^5 - 1$ and $6^3 \leq n \leq 6^4 - 1$ imply that $216 \leq n \leq 242$. Hence, there are 27 numbers satisfying the given conditions.

4. (C)
Notice that the largest 4-digit base-17 integer is $17^4 - 1$, which can be factorized into $(17^2 - 1)(17^2 + 1) = (16)(18)(290)$. Out of prime factors, 29 is the largest.

5. (C)
Given $\overline{abcd}_8$, there are 7 possible ways to choose a, 8 possible ways to choose b, c, and d, respectively. Therefore, there are $7 \times 8 \times 8 \times 8 = 3584$ number of ways to choose a, b, c, and d. Therefore, the answer is (C).

6. (E)
Notice that

$$\overline{1dd5}_{13} = 1 \cdot 13^3 + d \cdot 13^2 + d \cdot 13 + 5$$
$$= 1(12 + 1)^3 + d(12 + 1)^2 + d(12 + 1) + 5$$
$$= 12K + (1 + d + d + 5)$$

for some large integer K. All we need to know is that $2d + 6$ is a multiple of 12, where $d \in \{0, 1, 2, 3, \cdots, 12\}$. By plugging back and forth, we can easily find out that $d = 3, 9$. Therefore, the product of these two values is 27.

7. (C)
First, a single digit expression $A_9 = A_{17}$ implies that $A = \{1, 2, 3, \cdots, 8\}$. Second, a two-digit expression $AB_9 = BA_{17}$ implies that $8A = 16B$, so $(A, B) = (2, 1), (4, 2), (6, 3), (8, 4)$. Third, a three-digit expression $ABC_9 = CBA_{17}$ implies that $10A = 36C + B$, so $(A, B, C) = (4, 4, 1), (8, 8, 2)$. Assume that it is true for a four-digit integer. Then,

$\overline{ABCD}_9 = \overline{DCBA}_{17}$ implies that $4913D + 289C + 17B + A = 729A + 81B + 9C + D$. Simplify it into $614D + 35C = 91A + 8B$. Now, $2(307D - 4B) = 7(13A - 5C)$. Assume $D = 1$. Then, $307D - 4B = 307, 303, 299, 295, 291, 287, 283, 279$, and 275. Since 287 is divisible by 7, we must solve for $13A - 5C = 82$. Here, there exists no (A, C) satisfying $13A - 5C = 82$. Manually, we can check that there is no more expression in base-9 and base-17 equal in five or more digits. It can be provable but it takes a while. Hence, there are 14 integers in total.

8. (E)

$$\overline{X8Z9}_{17} = X(17)^3 + 8(17)^2 + Z(17) + 9$$
$$= X(18-1)^3 + 8(18-1)^2 + Z(18-1) + 9$$
$$= 18K + (-X + 8 - Z + 9)$$
$$= 18K + (17 - X - Z)$$
$$= 18K + (X + Z - 17)$$

We need to make sure $X + Z - 17$ is a multiple of 18. In other words, $X + Z - 17 = 0$, $X + Z - 17 = 18$, $X + Z - 17 = 36$, and so on. The first one makes sense, but others will not make sense since $X, Z \leq 16$. Therefore, $X + Z = 17$ implies that $(X, Z) = (16, 1), \cdots, (1, 16)$. We exclude $(17, 0)$ and $(0, 17)$ because 17 is not allowed in base-17 expression as a single digit. Therefore, there are 16 pairs of (X, Z).

9. (C)
$\overline{ABC}_7 = \overline{CB}_{12}$ implies that $49A + 7B + C = 12C + B$, so $49A + 6B = 11C$. Here, $(A, B, C) = (1, 1, 5)$ is the only solution. $n = 115_7 = 51_{12} = 61$. The answer is (C).

10. (A)
The first condition can turn into $a = b + 1$. The second condition turns into $b^2 = 5a + 1$ where $b^2 = 5(b+1) + 1 = 5b + 6$, so $b^2 - 5b - 6 = 0$ implies that $b = 6$. Therefore, $a = b + 1 = 6 + 1 = 7$. The answer is (A).

11. (D)
The first condition can be paraphrased into $16^3 \leq n < 16^4$. Hence, $2^{12} \leq n < 2^{16}$ implies that n has 13, 14, 15, and 16 digits. Hence, $13 + 14 + 15 + 16 = 58$ is the answer.

12. (D)
The thermometer uses base-9, so $139_{10} = 164_9$ implies that the sum of digits that appear in the false thermometer is 11. The answer is (D).

13. (E)

Notice that $2021 = 2025 - 4 = 9 \cdot 15^2 - 4 = 8(15^2) + 14(15) + 11$. Thus, a single-digit palindrome can be written as A_{15} where $A \in \{1, 2, 3, \cdots, 14\}$. Two-digit palindromes can be written as AA_{15} where $A \in \{1, 2, 3, \cdots, 14\}$. Likewise, three-digit palindrome can be written as ABA_{15} where $A \in \{1, 2, 3, \cdots, 8\}$ and $B \in \{0, 1, 2, \cdots, 14\}$. Hence, there are $14 + 14 + 120 = 148$ palindromes satisfying the given condition.

14. (D)

Check that $399 = 7^3 + 7^2 + 7^1$. Thus, 399 must be in $\overline{1110}_2$th position, according to the patterns we notice from the given sequence. Thus, $n = 8 + 4 + 2 = 14$ is the answer.

15. (C)

The remainder when the given number is divided by 16 equals the remainder when the sum of digits of the original number is divided by 16. This is always true if we deal with a number in base-N to be divided out by $N - 1$. Hence, when $45(= 1 + 2 + \cdots + 9)$ is divided by 16, the remainder is equal to 13.

16. (C)

First, $8 + 7 + A + B$ is a multiple of 3 and $B = 5, 0$. If $B = 0$, then $A = 0, 3, 6, 9$. Similarly, if $B = 5$, then $A = 1, 4, 7$. Hence, there are 7 pairs of (A, B).

17. (A)

First, $4^1 \leq n \leq 4^2 - 1$ and $5^1 \leq n \leq 5^2 - 1$ imply that $n = 10, 11, 12, 13, 14, 15$, since n is a two-digit number. Likewise, $4^2 \leq n \leq 4^3 - 1$ and $5^2 \leq n \leq 5^3 - 1$ imply that $n = 25, 26, \cdots, 63$. Therefore, there are 45 values of n, in total.

18. (C)

The original number and the sum of its digits has the same remainder when it is divided by 9. Hence, $S(1234\cdots20) = S(210) = S(3) = 3$. Therefore, the answer is (C).

19. (D)

$9 \times \overline{BC} = \overline{ABC}$ implies that $20B + 2C = 25A$. The only triples that work out are $(A, B, C) = (2, 2, 5), (4, 5, 0)$, and $(6, 7, 5)$. Thus, there are three triples satisfying the original condition.

20. (E)

Using complementary counting, we get $4 \times 5^4 - 4 \times 4 \times 3 \times 2 \times 1 = 2404$. Therefore, the answer is (E).

Did you know?

1. Qin Jiushao, a Chinese mathematician, developed Chinese Remainder Theorem, based on his experience in the Army in the 13th century. This method was rediscovered by Ruffini and Horner in Europe in the 19th century.

2. Dirichlet, famous for pigeonhole principle, proved Fermat's Last Theorem for $n = 5$ and $n = 14$.

3. Ramanujan came up with partition function, which we also learn in counting and probability.

4. Lagrange proved that every positive integer is the sum of four squares of integers.

5. Atle Selberg and Paul Erdos gave the first proof of the prime number theorem, stating that the density of primes become scarce as numbers get large.

6. The average gap between consecutive prime numbers among the first N integers is roughly $\log(N)$ in base 10.

7. Fermat's famous Last Theorem was first discovered by his son in the margin in his father's copy of an edition of Diophantus, where he wrote that the margin was too small to include the proof. Nobody knows whether he really proved it, but the proof of his last theorem by Andrew Wiles is 129 pages long, so most mathematicians doubt Fermat's claim.

8. Professor Terence Tao, who received Fields medal in 2006, with Professor Green proved that it is always possible to find, somewhere in the infinity of integers, a progression of prime numbers of equal spacing and any length.

TOPIC 5

Modular Arithmetic

5.1 Basic Knowledge of Modular Arithmetic

First, let n be an integer. Then, for any positive integer d, there exists a unique value of r such that

$$n = dq + r \text{ where } 0 \leq r < d$$
$$n \equiv r \pmod{d}$$

Here, the two equations are paraphrasable. As we use modular arithmetic, or modulo residue system, we can solve numerous number theory questions in math contests by using

- simplification by factorization
- inverse elements

Example Simplify $4x \equiv 6 \pmod{12}$.

Step-by-step Solution
#1. Since 4, 6 and 12 have a common factor of 2, divide all numbers by 2.
#2. Hence, $2x \equiv 3 \pmod{6}$.

Example Simplify $4x \equiv 6 \pmod{27}$.

Step-by-step Solution
#1. Since 4 and 6 have a common factor of 2, but 27 has no factor of 2, leave 27 alone.
#2. Hence, $2x \equiv 3 \pmod{27}$.

Now, as we look at inverse elements, we use the following equation set-up to find out inverse elements.

$$a \cdot a^{-1} \equiv 1 \pmod{n} \text{ if } a \text{ and } n \text{ are relatively prime.}$$

Example Find the value of $3^{-1} \pmod{7}$.

Step-by-step Solution
#1. Notice that 3 is relatively prime to 7, so 3^{-1} exists.
#2. $3 \cdot 3^{-1} \equiv 1 \pmod{7}$, so let $n = 3^{-1}$ to write $3n \equiv 1 \pmod{7}$.
#3. Since $5(3n) \equiv 5 \pmod{7}$, we get $15n \equiv 5 \pmod{7}$.
#4. Since $15 \equiv 1 \pmod{7}$, we conclude that $n \equiv 3^{-1} \equiv 5 \pmod{7}$.

Basic Drill 10

1. Find the smallest positive value of n satisfying $3n \equiv 12 \pmod{27}$.

2. Find the smallest positive value of n satisfying $3n \equiv 6 \pmod 8$.

3. Find the value of $4^{-1} \pmod 9$.

4. Find the value of $5^{-1} \pmod 7$.

Answer to Basic Drill 10

1.

$$3n \equiv 12 \pmod{27}$$
$$n \equiv 4 \pmod 9$$
$$n = 9k + 4$$

This implies that $\boxed{4}$ is the smallest positive integer value of n satisfying $3n \equiv 12 \pmod{27}$.

2.

$$3n \equiv 6 \pmod 8$$
$$n \equiv 2 \pmod 9$$
$$n = 8k + 2$$

This implies that $\boxed{2}$ is the smallest positive integer value of n satisfying $3n \equiv 6 \pmod 8$.

3.

$$4 \cdot 4^{-1} \equiv 1 \pmod 9$$
$$7(4 \cdot 4^{-1}) \equiv 7 \pmod 9$$
$$28 \cdot 4^{-1} \equiv 7 \pmod 9$$
$$4^{-1} \equiv \boxed{7} \pmod 9$$

4.

$$5 \cdot 5^{-1} \equiv 1 \pmod 7$$
$$3(5 \cdot 5^{-1}) \equiv 3 \pmod 7$$
$$15 \cdot 5^{-1} \equiv 3 \pmod 7$$
$$5^{-1} \equiv \boxed{3} \pmod 7$$

Practice

1. Let $n \equiv (5^{-1} + 7^{-1})^{-1} \pmod{11}$. What is the remainder when n is divided by 11?

(A) 1
(B) 2
(C) 3
(D) 4
(E) 5

2. For how many integers n satisfying $1 \leq n \leq 17$ is it true that $n \equiv n^{-1} \pmod{18}$?

(A) 2
(B) 3
(C) 4
(D) 5
(E) 6

3. 997 is the largest three-digit prime integer. Which of the following is the correct value of the following expression?

$$1^{-1} \cdot 2^{-1} + 2^{-1} \cdot 3^{-1} + 3^{-1} \cdot 4^{-1} + \cdots + 995^{-1} \cdot 996^{-1} \pmod{997}$$

(A) 0
(B) 1
(C) 2
(D) 3
(E) 4

4. Find the sum of the digits of the smallest positive integer n such that $n^{-1} \pmod{102}$ and $n^{-1} \pmod{119}$ do not exist.
(A) 2
(B) 3
(C) 4
(D) 5
(E) 8

5. Let n be a positive integer. If 7 is its own inverse in residue modulo n, but 5 is not its own inverse in residue modulo n, although 5^{-1} does exist, how many possible values for n are between 1 and 49, inclusive?

(A) 2
(B) 3
(C) 4
(D) 5
(E) 6

6. Given that k is a positive integer less than 12, how many values can k take on such that $4n \equiv k \pmod{12}$ has no solution in $n \in \mathbb{Z}$?

(A) 3
(B) 6
(C) 9
(D) 10
(E) 11

7. "Number Theory ∞" is a hypothetical math prepbook with somewhat large number of chapters with 20 questions per chapter, but Bob solves 12 questions a day. After a large number of days passed since he started solving questions in this prepbook from the beginning without skipping a single question, Bob noticed that he needed to solve 4 more problems to complete the very chapter in which he was solving questions. Which of the following could be the number of days passed since he started solving questions?
(A) 2021
(B) 2022
(C) 2023
(D) 2024
(E) 2025

8. The number of Bob's stamps is a multiple of 6. When he loses two of them, the number of stamps he collected so far turns into a multiple of n. If n is a positive even integer less than 20, then how many possible values are there for n?
(A) 4
(B) 5
(C) 6
(D) 7
(E) 8

9. If a book has 200 pages with the same number of words per page, and Bob reads 505 words per day. At his last day of reading, he only read 175 words to finish the whole book. Assuming that there are at least 400 words yet at most 500 words per page, if the number of words per page is $\overline{abc}_{10}$, find the sum of a, b, and c.
(A) 12
(B) 14
(C) 16
(D) 18
(E) 20

10. Bo thought of a number that is a positive multiple of 6. If he subtracts one, the number turns into a multiple of n. If n is a positive integer less than or equal to 2022, how many possible values of n are there?
(A) 673
(B) 674
(C) 675
(D) 676
(E) 677

Answer Key from 1 to 10

1. (B)

First, $9 \cdot 5 \equiv 1 \pmod{11}$ implies that $5^{-1} \equiv 9 \pmod{11}$. Likewise, $7 \cdot 8 \equiv 1 \pmod{11}$ implies that $7^{-1} \equiv 8 \pmod{11}$. Therefore, $n \equiv (9+8)^{-1} \equiv 17^{-1} \equiv 6^{-1} \equiv 2 \pmod{11}$.

2. (A)

In order for n^{-1} to exist in residue modulo 18, n must be relatively prime to 18. If n is relatively prime to 18, then $n = 1, 5, 7, 11, 13, 17$. Manually checking all the answers, we get $n = 1, 17$ are the only solutions that work.

3. (C)

Similar to $1/(n(n+1)) = 1/n - 1/(n+1)$, we get the following identity $n^{-1}(n+1)^{-1} \equiv n^{-1} - (n+1)^{-1} \pmod{p}$. Hence, the given expression turns into $1^{-1} - 996^{-1} \equiv 1 - (-1) \equiv 2 \pmod{997}$ by terms eliminated in alternating sum and difference.

4. (D)

Notice that $a^{-1} \pmod{n}$ is undefined if a and n are NOT relatively prime. Since $102 = 2 \cdot 3 \cdot 17$, write down the list of positive integers that are not relatively prime to 102, i.e., $\{2, 3, 4, 6, 8, 9, 10, 12, 14, 15, 16, 17, \cdots\}$. Likewise, since $119 = 7 \cdot 17$, write down the list of positive integers that are not relatively prime to 119, i.e., $\{7, 14, 17, \cdots\}$. Since the smallest integer common to both sets is 14, the sum of its digit equals 5.

5. (A)

Since 7 is its own inverse in mod n, it means that $49 \equiv 1 \pmod{n}$, so $48 \pmod{n}$. In other words, we are looking at positive divisors of $48 = 2^4 \cdot 3^1$. There are 10 possible values of n. On the other hand, 5 is not its own inverse in n, which means that $25 \not\equiv 1 \pmod{n}$. Hence, $24 \not\equiv 0 \pmod{n}$. Then, $n = 16, 48$. There are only two values.

6. (C)

Observe that the leftside of the modular equation is a multiple of 4. Hence, if $k = 4q + 1$, $4q + 2$, and $4q + 3$ for some q, then $4n \equiv k \pmod{12}$ turns into $4n = 12k + 4q + 1$, $12k + 4q + 2$ and $12k + 4q + 3$, respectively. Since the left-side is a multiple of 4 whereas the right-side is not, we conclude that there are 9 values of k, i.e., $\{1, 2, 3, 5, 6, 7, 9, 10, 11\}$.

7. (C)

Let n be the number of days passed since he began to solve questions in the book. Then, $12n \equiv -4 \equiv 16 \pmod{20}$. This implies that $3n \equiv 2 \pmod{5}$. Thus, $n \equiv 3 \pmod{5}$. Out of the answer choices, 2023 is the only integer whose remainder is 3 when divided by 5.

8. (C)

Let $6k$ be the number of stamps Bob has. According to the given condition, $6k - 2 \equiv 0$ (mod n). Hence, $6k \equiv 2$ (mod n). Since $n \in \{2, 4, 6, 8, 10, 12, 14, 16, 18\}$, if n is a multiple of 6, then there exists no integer k satisfying the given condition. Hence, eliminate 6, 12, and 18. Thus, there are 6 different values of n.

9. (D)

Let n be the number of words in a single page. Then,

$$200n \equiv 175 \pmod{505}$$
$$40n \equiv 35 \pmod{101}$$
$$8n \equiv 7 \pmod{101}$$
$$104n \equiv 91 \pmod{101}$$
$$3n \equiv 91 \pmod{101}$$
$$3n \equiv 192 \pmod{101}$$
$$n \equiv 64 \pmod{101}$$

Hence, $n \in \{64, 165, 266, 367, 468, \cdots\}$. Conclude that $468 = \overline{abc}$, so $a + b + c = 4 + 6 + 8 = 18$.

10. (B)

In a nutshell, $6k \equiv 1$ (mod n) has a solution $k > 0$ for some n. This means that 6 and n are relatively prime. Thus, n is not divisible by 2 nor 3. By principle of inclusion and exclusion, we get $2022 - (2022/2 + 2022/3 - 2022/6) = 2022 - 1011 - 674 + 337 = 674$. (Normally, we use floor function, but 2022 is divisible by 2, 3, and 6.)

5.2 Application of Modular Arithmetic

There are numerous applications of modular arithmetic. The Chinese Remainder Theorem, also known as CRT, which solves a system of modular equations, can be directly applied as a word problem or as a remainder equation. Extending the idea of CRT, we may solve quadratic equations in residue modulo n. That being written, we are ready to talk about Fermat's Little Theorem and Euler's Theorem, a generalized version of Fermat's Little Theorem.

Example Find the smallest positive value of n satisfying $n \equiv 2 \pmod 3$ and $n \equiv 3 \pmod 4$.

Step-by-step Solution
#1. First, write the first few values of $n \equiv 2 \pmod 3$, i.e., $\{2, 5, 8, 11, 14, 17, \cdots\}$.
#2. Likewise, find the first few values of $n \equiv 3 \pmod 4$, i.e., $\{3, 7, 11, 15, \cdots\}$.
#3. Out of common values, the smallest value is 11, so we conclude 11 is the smallest.

Example Find the smallest positive value of n satisfying $n \equiv 4 \pmod 7$ and $n \equiv 5 \pmod 8$.

Step-by-step Solution
#1. Choose the modular equation with larger base and change it into a long-division form, i.e., $n = 8k + 5$ for some integer k.
#2. Substitute $n = 8k + 5$ into the first equation to get $8k + 5 \equiv 4 \pmod 7$, so $8k \equiv -1 \pmod 7$. Hence, $k \equiv 6 \pmod 7$.
#3. Convert $k \equiv 6 \pmod 7$ into $k = 7q + 6$, and replace it into $n = 8k + 5$, i.e., $n = 8(7q + 6) + 5 = 56q + 48 + 5 = 56q + 53$.
#4. Hence, the smallest positive value of n satisfying the two equations is 53.

Since many number theory problems involve remainder questions involving chinese remainder theorem, we must have another tool of finding a remainder quickly without computing from A to Z. We begin with Fermat's Little Theorem with a prime base p. In particular, if $a > 0$ is relatively prime to p,

$$a^{p-1} \equiv 1 \pmod p$$

Example Find the remainder when 3^{2025} is divided by 47.

Step-by-step Solution
#1. By Fermat's Little Theorem, we notice that $3^{46} \equiv 1 \pmod{47}$.
#2. Since 2025 is larger than 46, divide it out by 46 to conclude that $2021 = 46(44) + 1$.
#3. Rewrite $3^{2025} = 3^{46(44)+1} = 3^{46(44)} \cdot 3^1 \equiv 1 \cdot 3 \equiv 3 \pmod{47}$.
#4. Conclude that the remainder when 3^{2025} is divided by 47 is 3.

What if the base is not prime? What happens if the base is given by any positive integer n? Then, Euler's theorem states that, if a is relatively prime to n,

$$a^{\phi(n)} \equiv 1 \pmod{n} \text{ where } \phi(n) \text{ is the number of relatively prime positive}$$
$$\text{integers to } n, \text{ less than or equal to } n.$$

If $n = p_1^{q_1} p_2^{q_2} \cdots p_k^{q_k}$ where $k \geq 1$, then $\phi(n) = n(1 - 1/p_1)(1 - 1/p_2) \cdots (1 - 1/p_k)$, which is a direct result of the principle of inclusion and exclusion. Have a look at a following example to justify why this must be true.

Example Compute $\phi(10)$, where ϕ is Euler's totient function.

Step-by-step Solution
#1. Since $10 = 2 \cdot 5$, find out the number of multiples of 2 or 5.
#2. There are 5 multiples of 2 and 2 multiples of 5, where a multiple of 10 is overcounted.
#3. By the principle of inclusion and exclusion, we retrieve $10 - (5 + 2 - 1)$.
#4. Check out that

$$10(1 - 1/2)(1 - 1/5) = 10(1 - 1/2 - 1/5 + 1/10)$$
$$= 10 - 5 - 2 + 1$$
$$= 10 - (5 + 2 - 1)$$

If a is not relatively prime to n, then we must find another clever way of reducing the size of a compared to n. Let's have a look at simple example.

Example Find the remainder when 7^{2025} is divided by 48.

Step-by-step Solution
#1. Notice that 48 is not a prime number. Compute $\phi(48) = 48(1 - 1/2)(1 - 1/3) = 16$.
#2. Since $2025 = 16(126) + 9$, we conclude that $7^{2025} \equiv 7^9 \equiv 49^4 \cdot 7 \equiv 7 \mod 48$.
#3. The remainder is 7.

Example Find the remainder when 3^{2025} is divided by 48.

Step-by-step Solution
#1. First, 3 and 48 are not relatively prime.
#2. Notice that $3^4 \equiv 81 \equiv 33 \pmod{48}$, so $33^{505} \cdot 3 \equiv 3 \pmod{48}$ by checking a few computations.
#3. Conclude that $3^{2025} \equiv 3 \pmod{48}$.

Basic Drill 11

1. Compute the smallest positive value of n satisfying

$$\begin{cases} n \equiv 2 \pmod{3} \\ n \equiv 3 \pmod{4} \end{cases}$$

2. Compute the smallest positive value of n satisfying

$$\begin{cases} 2n + 1 \equiv 4 \pmod{7} \\ 3n - 1 \equiv 2 \pmod{11} \end{cases}$$

3. Find the value of $4^{15} \pmod 9$.

4. Find the value of $11^{11^{11}} \pmod{12}$.

Answer to Basic Drill 11

1.

First, $n \equiv 3 \pmod 4$ implies that $n = 4k+3$ for some integer k. Then, $4k+3 \equiv 2 \pmod 3$ implies that $k \equiv 2 \pmod 3$. Hence, $k = 3q+2$ for some integer q. Put it back into $n = 4k+3$ so that $n = 4(3q+2)+3 = 12q+11$. Therefore, the smallest positive value of n is $\boxed{11}$.

2. First, $2n \equiv 3 \pmod 7$ implies that $n \equiv 5 \pmod 7$. Likewise, $3n \equiv 3 \pmod{11}$ implies that $n \equiv 1 \pmod{11}$. Since $n \equiv 5 \pmod 7$ indicates that $n \in \{5, 12, 19, \cdots\}$, we can easily find out that the smallest positive value of n is $\boxed{12}$.

3.

$$4^{\phi(9)} \equiv 1 \pmod 9$$
$$4^6 \equiv 1 \pmod 9$$
$$4^{15} \equiv 4^3 \pmod 9$$
$$64 \equiv \boxed{1} \pmod 9$$

4.

Since $11 \equiv -1 \pmod{12}$, we get $(-1)^{\text{odd}} \equiv -1 \equiv 11 \pmod{12}$. Hence, the remainder when $11^{11^{11}}$ is divided by 12 is $\boxed{11}$.

Practice

11. The number of apples Bob bought can be counted in two methods. As he packed five apples as one bundle, he was left with three leftover apples. On the other hand, if he packed seven apples as one bundle, he was left with two leftover apples. If it is known that the number of apples he bought is more than 100 apples, which of the following is the sum of the digits of the smallest possible number of apples he could have bought?

(A) 10
(B) 11
(C) 12
(D) 13
(E) 14

12. Daniel bought some number of boxes of chocolate chips. Each box normally contains 12 chips. When he took all the chips out and bundles them into groups of 7, he had two chips left over. If he bought more than 10 boxes, yet less than 100 boxes, compute the total number of boxes he could have bought.

(A) 10
(B) 11
(C) 12
(D) 13
(E) 14

13. Compute the remainder when $1^{19} + 2^{19} + 3^{19} + \cdots + 100^{19}$ is divided by 19.

(A) 11
(B) 12
(C) 13
(D) 14
(E) 15

14. Compute the units digit of $7^{7^{7^{7^{7^{7^{7^{7^{7}}}}}}}}$.

(A) 1
(B) 2
(C) 3
(D) 4
(E) 5

15. If Bob stacks his coins in piles of 5, he has 3 left over. Likewise, if he stacks his coins in piles of 7, he has 4 left over. Lastly, if he stacks his coins in piles of 11, he has 6 left over. Compute the sum of the first two smallest number of coins Bob may have.
(A) 721
(B) 731
(C) 751
(D) 771
(E) 791

16. Compute the number of n such that $1 \leq n \leq 25$ and "$\phi(n)$ is a factor of n," where $\phi(n)$ is the number of positive integers less than or equal to n which are coprime to n.
(A) 3
(B) 5
(C) 7
(D) 9
(E) 11

17. Let $n = \overline{1357911131517\cdots 2021}$. Compute the remainder when n is divided by 72.

(A) 27
(B) 36
(C) 45
(D) 54
(E) 63

18. Suppose that a 2021-digit integer N consists of 1011 number of 9's and 1010 number of 5's. Compute the remainder when N is divided by 36.

(A) 15
(B) 17
(C) 19
(D) 21
(E) 23

19. Assuming that $n > 0$, if 2 divides n, 3 divides $n+1$, 4 divides $n+2$, 5 divides $n+3$, compute the number of n less than or equal to 2021.
(A) 31
(B) 32
(C) 33
(D) 34
(E) 35

20. If $n^2 - 4n + 3 \equiv 0 \pmod{91}$, where $1 \leq n < 91$, compute the sum of all possible solutions to the quadratic modular equation.
(A) 95
(B) 97
(C) 99
(D) 101
(E) 103

Answer Key from 11 to 20

11. (B)

We are solving the following system of modular equations.

$$\begin{cases} n \equiv 3 \pmod{5} \\ n \equiv 2 \pmod{7} \end{cases}$$

First, $n = 7k + 2$ for some k. Then, $7k + 2 \equiv 3 \pmod{5}$ implies that $k \equiv 3 \pmod{5}$, so $k = 5q + 3$ for some integer q. Hence, $n = 7(5q + 3) + 2 = 35q + 23$. Thus, $n \in \{23, 58, 93, 128, \cdots\}$. Since we are looking for the smallest 3-digit positive integer, we conclude that $n = 128$. We are looking for the sum of its digits, so it must be $11 = 1 + 2 + 8$.

12. (D)

Let n be the number of boxes of chocolate chips Daniel bought. Then, $12n \equiv 2 \pmod{7}$, which is equivalent to $6n \equiv 1 \pmod{7}$, we conclude that $n \equiv 6 \pmod{7}$. According to the original condition, $10 < n < 100$ implies that $n \in \{13, 20, \cdots, 97\}$ where $13 = 7 \cdot 1 + 6$ and $97 = 7 \cdot 13 + 6$. By 1-to-1 correspondence, there are 13 possible values of n.

13. (E)

By Fermat's Little Theorem, $a^{p-1} \equiv 1 \pmod{p}$ if a and p are relatively prime and p is a prime number. Hence, $a^p \equiv a \pmod{p}$ with the same condition. On the other hand, if a is a multiple of p, then $a^p \equiv 0 \pmod{p}$. Hence,

$$1^{19} + 2^{19} + \cdots + 100^{19} = (1 + 2 + 3 + \cdots + 100) - (19 + 38 + 57 + 76 + 95)$$
$$= 5050 - 19K$$
$$\equiv 5050 \pmod{19}$$

Therefore, $5050 \equiv 15 \pmod{19}$ implies that the remainder is 15.

14. (C)

First, 10 is not prime. Hence, we cannot use Fermat's Little Theorem. This indicates that we must use Euler's Theorem. According to the theorem, $7^{\phi(10)} \equiv 1 \pmod{10}$, where $\phi(10) = 10(1 - 1/2)(1 - 1/5) = 4$. Now, we must see what the exponent results in when it is divided by 4. Notice that $3^{\text{odd}} \equiv (-1)^{\text{odd}} \equiv 3 \pmod{4}$. Thus, the original expression turns into $7^3 \equiv 3 \pmod{10}$.

TOPIC_5 Modular Arithmetic

15. (D)

We are solving

$$\begin{cases} n \equiv 3 \pmod{5} \\ n \equiv 4 \pmod{7} \\ n \equiv 6 \pmod{11} \end{cases}$$

Convert the third equation into $n = 11k + 6$. Then, $11k + 6 \equiv 4 \pmod{7}$ implies that $k \equiv 3 \pmod{7}$. Convert it into $k = 7q + 3$, and put it back into the $n = 11k + 6$ to conclude that $n = 77q + 39$. Now, put it into the first equation to get $77q + 39 \equiv 3 \pmod{5}$. Hence, $2q \equiv 4 \pmod{5}$, so $q \equiv 2 \pmod{5}$. Convert it into $q = 5x + 2$. Put it back into $n = 77q + 39$ to conclude $n = 385x + 193$. Therefore, $n \in \{193, 578, \cdots\}$. The sum of these two numbers is 771.

16. (D)

Observe that $1, 2, 4, 6, 8, 12, 16, 18, 24$ work by manually checking the answers. As you notice from the values that work, the integer in the form of $2^a 3^b$ does satisfy the condition. Let $n = 2^a 3^b$. Then, $\phi(n) = 2^a 3^b (1 - 1/2)(1 - 1/3) = 2^{a-1} \cdot 2 \cdot 3^{b-1} = 2^a 3^{b-1}$. Since $2^a 3^{b-1}$ always divides $2^a 3^b$, we conclude that there are 9 different values of n that satisfy the given condition. If there is other prime than 2 or 3, then $(1 - 1/p) = (p-1)/p$ indicates that $p - 1$ must be even number, possibly composite number, such that there are extra exponents in the $\phi(n)$'s prime factors compared to those in n.

17. (C)

As a typical Chinese Remainder Theorem, we tackle the question in mod 8 and 9. First, $1 + 3 + 5 + \cdots + 2021 = \frac{1011(1+2021)}{2} = 1011 \cdot 1011 \equiv 0 \pmod{9}$. Second, $n \equiv 5 \pmod{8}$ since $n = 1000k + 21$ for some large k. Let $n = 9q$ for some integer q. Then, $9q \equiv 5 \pmod{8}$ implies that $q \equiv 5 \pmod{8}$. Thus, $q = 8p + 5$ for some integer p. Thus, $n = 9q = 9(8q + 5) = 72q + 45$. Therefore, $n \equiv 45 \pmod{72}$.

18. (C)

First, $n \equiv 1 \pmod{9}$ in whichever arrangement of the given numbers, since the sum of the digits does not change in any configuration of the given digits. Second, have a look at the last two digits, possibly 59, 55, 99, and 95. In any of the four possibilities, we get the remainder of 3 when divided by 4. Thus, we are solving

$$\begin{cases} n \equiv 1 \pmod{9} \\ n \equiv 3 \pmod{4} \end{cases}$$

Let $n = 9k + 1$ for some k. Hence, $9k + 1 \equiv 3 \pmod{4}$ implies that $k \equiv 2 \pmod{4}$, which can be paraphrased into $k = 4q + 2$. Put it back into the first set-up such that $n = 9(4q + 2) + 1 = 36q + 19$, i.e., $n \equiv 19 \pmod{36}$. Hence, the remainder is 19.

19. (D)

We are solving

$$\begin{cases} n \equiv 0 \pmod{2} \\ n \equiv -1 \pmod{3} \\ n \equiv -2 \pmod{4} \\ n \equiv -3 \pmod{5} \end{cases}$$

which can turn into

$$\begin{cases} n \equiv 2 \pmod{3} \\ n \equiv 2 \pmod{4} \\ n \equiv 2 \pmod{5} \end{cases}$$

This results ino $n \equiv 2 \pmod{60}$. Also, notice that $60(33) + 2 < 2021$, but $60(34) + 2 > 2021$. Hence, $60(0) + 2, 60(1) + 2, \cdots, 60(33) + 2$ are the numbers that are less than 2021 satisfying the original condition. Hence, there are 34 numbers in total.

20. (C)

Notice that $n^2 - 4n + 3 \equiv 0 \pmod{91}$ can turn into $(n-1)(n-3) \equiv 0 \pmod{91}$, so $n = 1$, 3. Now, for the remaining n-values, we must set

$$\text{either} \begin{cases} n - 1 \equiv 0 \pmod{7} \\ n - 3 \equiv 0 \pmod{13} \end{cases} \text{or} \begin{cases} n - 1 \equiv 0 \pmod{13} \\ n - 3 \equiv 0 \pmod{7} \end{cases}$$

First, $n \equiv 1 \pmod{7}$ and $n \equiv 3 \pmod{13}$ imply that $n = 91k + 29$ for some integer k. Second, $n \equiv 1 \pmod{13}$ and $n \equiv 3 \pmod{7}$ imply that $n = 91k' + 66$ for some integer k'. Therefore, $n = 1, 3, 29, 66$. Hence, the sum of all these numbers is 99.

Math Summer Programs
suggested by MIT

Applicants at MIT have participated in

- AwesomeMath

- Canada/USA Mathcamp

- Hampshire College Summer Studies in Mathematics (HCSSiM)

- Texas State Mathworks Honors Summer Math Camp

- MathILY

- Program in Mathematics for Young Scientists (PROMYS)

- The Ross Program

- Stanford University Mathematics Camp (SUMaC)

- Prove It! Math Academy

Math Contests
other than AMC/AIME/USAMO/IMO

There are some math contests that highschool students may like such as

- American Regions Mathematics League (ARML)

- Purple Comet Math Meet (PCMM)

- Johns Hopkins Math Tournament (JHMT)

- Harvard-MIT Math Tournament (HMMT)

- The Berkeley Math Tournament (BMT)

- Caltech Harvey-Mudd Math Competition (CHMMC)

- Carnegie Mellon Informatics and Mathematics Competition (CMIMC)

- The Princeton University Mathematics Competition (PUMaC)

- Stanford Math Tournament (SUMO)

- Spirit of Math International Contest (with Stanford SMILE)

- Lehigh Math Meet (for ARML)

TOPIC 6

Mixed Practice

1. (Application of Chinese Remainder Theorem)

   If $n^3 \equiv 1 \pmod 9$, where $1 \leq n < 9$, find the number of all possible integer values of n.

   (A) 1

   (B) 2

   (C) 3

   (D) 4

   (E) 5

2. (Application of Fermat's Little Theorem)

   What is the remainder when 13^{2022} is divided by 5?

   (A) 0

   (B) 1

   (C) 2

   (D) 3

   (E) 4

3. (Application of Fermat's Little Theorem)

What is the residue of 9^{2020}, modulo 17?

(A) 1

(B) 4

(C) 9

(D) 13

(E) 16

4. (Finding Patterns)

The number $2^{2033} + 3^{2033}$ is a multiple of 5. Compute the sum of the tens digit and ones digit when it is divided by 100.

(A) 2

(B) 4

(C) 6

(D) 8

(E) 10

5. (Mod 100)

When the expression $(2^0)(2^1)(2^2)(2^3)\cdots(2^{99})(2^{100})$ is written as an integer, compute the sum of the tens digit and the ones digit.

(A) 0

(B) 2

(C) 4

(D) 6

(E) 8

6. (Application of Fermat's Little Theorem)

What is the remainder of 5^{2022} when it is divided by 7?

(A) 1

(B) 2

(C) 3

(D) 4

(E) 5

7. (Finding Remainder)

Find the remainder when $1 + 2 + 2^2 + 2^3 + \cdots + 2^{2022}$ is divided by 7.

(A) 0
(B) 1
(C) 2
(D) 3
(E) 4

8. (Extension of Divisibility)

Suppose A is an integer such that $0 \leq A \leq 14$, and $\overline{123456789A_{74}}$ is a multiple of 15. What is A?

(A) 1
(B) 2
(C) 3
(D) 4
(E) 5

9. (Finding Patterns)

Let there be two sequences recursively defined as follows :

$$a_0 = 0, \ a_1 = 1, \ a_n = a_{n-2} + b_{n-1} \text{ for } n \geq 2$$

$$b_0 = 1, \ b_1 = 2, \ b_n = a_{n-1} + b_{n-2} \text{ for } n \geq 2$$

What is the remainder when $a_{2020} + b_{2020}$ is divided by 7?

(A) 0
(B) 1
(C) 2
(D) 4
(E) 6

10. (Finding Patterns)

The infinite sequence $F = \{F_0, F_1, F_2, \ldots\}$ is defined as $F_0 = 0$, $F_1 = 1$, and $F_n = F_{n-2} + F_{n-1}$ for all integers $n > 1$. Compute the remainder when $F_{2022} + F_{2023} + F_{2024} + F_{2025} + F_{2026} + F_{2027}$ is divided by 7.

(A) 1
(B) 2
(C) 3
(D) 4
(E) 5

11. (Using Binomial Coefficients for Mod 100)

It is well-known that for a positive integer n,

$$(a+b)^n = \binom{n}{n}a^n b^0 + \binom{n}{n-1}a^{n-1}b^1 + \cdots + \binom{n}{1}a^1 b^{n-1} + \binom{n}{0}a^0 b^n$$

Compute the tens digit of 17^{2022}.

(A) 1

(B) 2

(C) 4

(D) 8

(E) 0

12. (Application of Least Common Multiple)

Jack and Jamie both run in a circular track of 100 meters length in the same direction. Jack's speed is $\frac{17}{5}$ meters per second, and Jamie's is $\frac{13}{3}$ meters per second. If they start at the same time, in how many minutes will they be at the starting point altogether for the first time?

(A) 20

(B) 25

(C) 30

(D) 35

(E) 40

13. (Application of Least Common Multiple)

The least common multiple of 28, 50, and n is 700. Compute the number of all possible positive values of n.

(A) 12

(B) 16

(C) 18

(D) 20

(E) 22

14. (Motivation for Modular Arithmetic)

Compute the number of integer solutions to $24n^2 - 2468n + 246810 = 24681012$.

(A) 0

(B) 1

(C) 2

(D) 3

(E) 4

15. (Repetition in Modular Arithmetic)

The following function $f : \mathbb{N} \cup \{0\} \longrightarrow \mathbb{N} \cup \{0\}$ is given by $f(x_1) = 2020$ and the recursive rule such that

$$f(n) = \begin{cases} \dfrac{n}{4} & (n \text{ is a multiple of } 4) \\ n - 1 & (n \text{ is not a multiple of } 4) \end{cases}$$

If $x_{n+1} = f(x_n)$ for $n \geq 1$, compute the largest $k \in \mathbb{N}$, such that $x_k \neq 0$.

(A) 14
(B) 15
(C) 16
(D) 17
(E) 18

16. (Repetition in Modular Arithmetic)

Let a and b be positive integers less than or equal to 99, and $a > b$. In how many pairs of (a, b) pairs will $ab + a + b \equiv 0 \pmod{3}$ be satisfied?

(A) 1024
(B) 1056
(C) 1240
(D) 1440
(E) 1842

17. (Application of Remainders)

Let A be the maximal number that uses distinct digits once and B be the minimum number that uses the distinct non-zero digits once. Compute the value of $A - B$ in residue modulo 37.

(A) 0

(B) 10

(C) 11

(D) 26

(E) 36

18. (Calendar in Mod 7)

Suppose you wish to make a new year's plan for 2022. You only have the calendar of year 2021. Which month of 2021 has exactly same date with 2022 January?

(A) January

(B) February

(C) March

(D) April

(E) May

19. (Finding Patterns)

Compute the remainder of when 11^{2022} is divided by 13.

(A) 8
(B) 9
(C) 10
(D) 11
(E) 12

20. (Properties of Multiples)

The price of 286 hardcover books equals $\overline{5A0B6}$ dollars, where A and B are nonzero digits, assuming that the price of one hardcover book does not change per book. Compute the sum of the digits of the price of one book.

(A) 15
(B) 16
(C) 17
(D) 18
(E) 19

21. (Integer Grids)

From $(0,0)$ to $(14,6)$, assume there is a straight line segment connecting two endpoints. Draw all the boundaries of each unit-square grid altogether so that there are grids that have intersection point(s) or not. In particular, we are interested in 84 unit grids, parallel to the given axes, filling up the rectangle whose diagonal is a segment from $(0,0)$ to $(14,6)$. How many 1×1 grids have at least one point of intersection with the line segment?

(A) 14
(B) 16
(C) 18
(D) 20
(E) 22

22. (Sum of Divisors)

If the sum of positive factors of 496 is given by $\overline{abc}_{10}$, compute the sum $a + b + c$.

(A) 14
(B) 16
(C) 18
(D) 20
(E) 22

23. (Divisors)

Let $P(n)$ for an integer n denote the largest proper divisor (possibly 1) of n. Compute the number of n satisfying $P(n) > P(2021)$ where $1 \leq n \leq 100$.

(A) 0
(B) 1
(C) 2
(D) 3
(E) 4

24. (Divisibility)

Compute the number of distinct 4-digit numbers that are divisible by 3 and the last two digits are 32.

(A) 27
(B) 30
(C) 33
(D) 36
(E) 39

25. (Geometry and Number Theory)

Given a right triangle ABC where $\angle B$ is right angle, if one of the sides is given by $\overline{AB}$ such that $AB = 30$, compute the number of possible lengths of circumradius, if the other side also has an integer side length and the diameter is also an integer.

(A) 0
(B) 1
(C) 2
(D) 3
(E) 4

Answer Key to 1 to 25

1. (C)
Since $n^3 \equiv 1 \pmod{9}$ can turn into $n^3 - 1 \equiv 0 \pmod{9}$, we can further factorize it into $(n-1)(n^2+n+1) \equiv 0 \pmod{9}$. If $n \equiv 1 \pmod{9}$, then the equation holds true. Suppose $n^2 + n + 1 \equiv 0 \pmod{9}$, then there exists some k such that $n \equiv k \pmod{9}$ such that $k^2 + k + 1 \equiv 0 \pmod{9}$. However, if we manually check all k values from 0 to 8, none of the values works. Hence, we conclude that there is no n satisfying $n^2 + n + 1 \equiv 0 \pmod{9}$. On the other hand, assume that $n - 1 \equiv 0 \pmod{3}$ and $n^2 + n + 1 \equiv 0 \pmod{3}$. Both equations hold true as long as $n \equiv 1 \pmod{3}$. Thus, $n \in \{1, 4, 7\}$ are solutions to the equation in the last assumption. Summing all these results into one, we conclude that $n = 1, 4, 7$ are the integer solutions to $n^3 \equiv 1 \pmod{9}$ for $1 \leq n < 9$.

2. (E)
Note that 13^{51} is $(10+3)^{51}$. Any term in the expansion that involves the 10 will be 0 modulo 5, so it suffices to consider $3^{51} \pmod 5$. We look for a pattern in powers of 3.

$$3^1 \equiv 3 \pmod 5$$
$$3^2 \equiv 4 \pmod 5$$
$$3^3 \equiv 2 \pmod 5$$
$$3^4 \equiv 1 \pmod 5.$$

Other than manual checking, we can use Fermat's Little Theorem. Notice that we are given with residue modulo prime. In other words, $a^{p-1} \equiv 1 \pmod p$ if a is relatively prime to p and p is a prime number. It is easy to check that $3^4 \equiv 1 \pmod 5$. However, we are not sure of the fact whether this is the smallest power of 3 that is 1 mod 5. However, the results above show that this is the smallest power. Hence, we see that $3^{2022} \equiv 3^2 \equiv 4 \pmod 5$, hence our desired remainder is 4.

3. (E)
Let's manually check the result by generating powers of 9 modulo 17. Note that we can generate 9^{2^k} by squaring 9^k. This is always useful because we can get a cycle of residuals in mod 17. We get

$$9^1 \equiv 9 \pmod{17}$$
$$9^2 \equiv 13 \pmod{17}$$
$$9^4 \equiv 16 \pmod{17}$$
$$9^8 \equiv 1 \pmod{17}.$$

Since $9^8 \equiv 1$ modulo 17, we have

$$9^{2020} \equiv 9^4 \pmod{17}$$
$$\equiv 81 \cdot 81 \pmod{17}$$
$$\equiv (-4) \cdot (-4) \pmod{17}$$
$$\equiv 16 \pmod{17}$$

4. (C)

We notice that after the first pair, the sequence repeats every 20. Have a look at the following set of equations.

$$2^1 + 3^1 \equiv 5 \pmod{100}$$
$$2^2 + 3^2 \equiv 13 \pmod{100}$$
$$2^3 + 3^3 \equiv 35 \pmod{100}$$
$$2^4 + 3^4 \equiv 97 \pmod{100}$$
$$2^5 + 3^5 \equiv 75 \pmod{100}$$
$$2^6 + 3^6 \equiv 93 \pmod{100}$$
$$2^7 + 3^7 \equiv 15 \pmod{100}$$
$$2^8 + 3^8 \equiv 17 \pmod{100}$$
$$2^9 + 3^9 \equiv 95 \pmod{100}$$
$$2^{10} + 3^{10} \equiv 73 \pmod{100}$$
$$2^{11} + 3^{11} \equiv 95 \pmod{100}$$
$$2^{12} + 3^{12} \equiv 37 \pmod{100}$$
$$2^{13} + 3^{13} \equiv 15 \pmod{100}$$
$$2^{14} + 3^{14} \equiv 53 \pmod{100}$$
$$2^{15} + 3^{15} \equiv 75 \pmod{100}$$
$$2^{16} + 3^{16} \equiv 57 \pmod{100}$$
$$2^{17} + 3^{17} \equiv 35 \pmod{100}$$
$$2^{18} + 3^{18} \equiv 33 \pmod{100}$$
$$2^{19} + 3^{19} \equiv 55 \pmod{100}$$
$$2^{20} + 3^{20} \equiv 77 \pmod{100}$$
$$2^{21} + 3^{21} \equiv 55 \pmod{100}$$
$$2^{22} + 3^{22} \equiv 13 \pmod{100}$$
$$2^{22} + 3^{22} \equiv 35 \pmod{100}$$

Therefore
$$2^{2033} + 3^{2033} \equiv 2^{13} + 3^{13} \equiv 15 \pmod{100}.$$

So, the sum of tens digit and ones digit is $1 + 5 = 6$.

5. (D)

Define the sequence

$$x_i = \text{the remainder when } 2^i \text{ is divided by } 100.$$

Then note that $x_{22} = x_2 = 4$, and thus this sequence repeats every 20 terms from x_2 onward. The desired product is $2^{1+2+3+\ldots+99+100} = 2^{5050}$. If we can find x_{5050}, we will then be done. But since $5050 = 20 \cdot 252 + 10$, we see that $x_{5050} = x_{10} = 24$. Thus our answer is $2 + 4 = 6$.

6. (A)

We start by writing out some powers of five modulo 7.

$$5^1 \equiv 5 \pmod 7$$
$$5^2 \equiv 4 \pmod 7$$
$$5^3 \equiv 6 \pmod 7$$
$$5^4 \equiv 2 \pmod 7$$
$$5^5 \equiv 3 \pmod 7$$
$$5^6 \equiv 1 \pmod 7$$

Therefore, we have that $5^6 \equiv 1$ modulo 7. Note that Fermat's Little Theorem can directly tell us that $5^{7-1} \equiv 1 \pmod 7$ since 5 and 7 are relatively prime. As shown in the list above, we can check that 5^6 is the first power of 5 that turns into 1 mod 7. Use $2022 \equiv 0 \pmod 6$, to conclude that $5^{2022} \equiv (5^6)^{337} \equiv 1^{335} \equiv 1$ modulo 7.

7. (B)

We look at the first few powers of 2 modulo 7:

$$2^0 \equiv 1,$$
$$2^1 \equiv 2,$$
$$2^2 \equiv 4,$$
$$2^3 \equiv 8 \equiv 1 \pmod 7$$

Since $2^3 \equiv 1 \pmod{7}$, the powers of 2 modulo 7 repeat in cycles of 3. Therefore,

$$1 + 2 + 2^2 + 2^3 + \cdots + 2^{2022}$$
$$\equiv 1 + 2 + 4 + 1 + 2 + 4 + \cdots + 1 + 2 + 4 + 1$$
$$\equiv (1 + 2 + 4) + (1 + 2 + 4) + \cdots + (1 + 2 + 4) + 1$$
$$\equiv 1 \pmod{7}.$$

8. (E)
Since $74 \equiv -1 \pmod{15}$, we can apply the divisibility test of 11 in mod 10. In particular, $1 - 2 + 3 - 4 + 5 - 6 + 7 - 8 + 9 - A \equiv 0 \pmod{15}$. Therefore, $5 - A \equiv 0 \pmod{15}$ implies that $A \equiv 5 \pmod{15}$. Since $0 \leq A \leq 14$, $A = 5$.

9. (D)
The problem is greatly simplified by defining the sequence $C = \{c_0, c_1, c_2, \ldots\}$ as $c_n = a_n + b_n$ for all nonnegative integers n. Then $c_0 = a_0 + b_0 = 0 + 1 = 1$ and $c_1 = a_1 + b_1 = 1 + 2 = 3$. Additionally, for integers $n > 1$ we have

$$c_n = a_n + b_n$$
$$= (a_{n-2} + b_{n-1}) + (a_{n-1} + b_{n-2})$$
$$= (a_{n-2} + b_{n-2}) + (a_{n-1} + b_{n-1})$$
$$= c_{n-2} + c_{n-1}.$$

Now, we can manually check that the remainder in residue modulo 7, we have a cycle of 16 integers such that $1, 3, 4, 0, 4, 4, 1, 5, 6, 4, 3, 0, 3, 3, 6, 2$ keep repeating. Since $c_{2020} \equiv c_4$, we get $c_{2020} \equiv 4 \pmod{7}$.

10. (C)
We need to find a pattern in F first. You may have heard of it by the name Fibonacci sequence. Reduced modulo 7 (we can still use the recurrence relation), it looks like

$$F \equiv \{0, 1, 1, 2, 3, 5, 1, 6, 0, 6, 6, 5, 4, 2, 6, 1, 0, 1 \ldots\}.$$

The first 16 terms are $\{0, 1, 1, 2, 3, 5, 1, 6, 0, 6, 6, 5, 4, 2, 6, 1\}$. As the next two are 0 and 1 and since the sequence is defined by recursion on the most recent two terms, the Fibonacci sequence modulo 7 consists of repetitions of $0, 1, 1, 2, 3, 5, 1, 6, 0, 6, 6, 5, 4, 2, 6, 1$. Since $F_{2022} = F_6$, we can easily conclude that $F_{2022} + F_{2023} + \cdots + F_{2027} = F_6 + F_7 + \cdots + F_{11}$, which is equal to $1 + 6 + 0 + 6 + 6 + 5 = 24 \equiv 3 \pmod{7}$.

11. (D)

$$(10+7)^{2022} \equiv \binom{2022}{1} \cdot 10^1 \cdot 7^{2021} + 7^{2022} \pmod{100}$$
$$\equiv 2022 \times 10 \times 7 + 49 \pmod{100}$$
$$\equiv 89 \pmod{100}$$

Here, $7^1 \equiv 7 \pmod{10}$, $7^2 \equiv 9 \pmod{10}$, $7^3 \equiv 3 \pmod{10}$, and $7^4 \equiv 1 \pmod{10}$. Likewise, $7^1 \equiv 7 \pmod{100}$, $7^2 \equiv 49 \pmod{100}$, $7^3 \equiv 43 \pmod{100}$, $7^4 \equiv 1 \pmod{100}$, and $7^5 \equiv 7 \pmod{100}$. The reason why we look at 7^{2021} in mod 10 is because the units digit of $2022 \times 10 \times 7^{2021}$ is 0. Hence, we only care about the tens digit from this term. On the other hand, 7^{2022} contribute both to units digit and tens digit. Computing the sum of all given numbers in mod 100, we get the tens digit as 8.

12. (B)

First, Jack spends $\frac{500}{17}$ seconds for one lap. In other words, for k seconds, Jack goes about $\frac{17k}{500}$ lap. Likewise, Jamie spends $\frac{300}{13}$ seconds for one lap. In other words, for k seconds, Jamie goes about $\frac{13k}{300}$ lap. Hence, in order for both to be at the starting point, k must be a least common multiple of 500 and 300. Hence, the smallest k must be 1500 seconds, which is 25 minutes.

13. (C)

First, $28 = 2^2 \cdot 7^1$, $50 = 2^1 \cdot 5^2$, and $n = 2^a \cdot 5^b \cdot 7^c$ since $700 = 2^2 \cdot 5^2 \cdot 7^1$. Hence, there are three choices for a since $0 \le a \le 2$, three choices for b since $0 \le b \le 2$, and two choices for c since $0 \le c \le 1$. Hence, there are 18 possible values of n.

14. (A)

Even integers can be categorized in two types in residue modulo 4. There are integers that are divisible by 4 or not. In fact, $\{0, 4, 8, 12, \cdots\}$ are always divisible by 4, whereas $\{2, 6, 10, 14, \cdots\}$ are not divisible by 4. Since $24n^2 - 2468n = 24681012 - 246810$ implies that $4K = 4Q + 2$ for some large integer K and Q, and we know that $0 \not\equiv 2 \pmod 4$, there is no integer solution satisfying the given equation.

15. (C)

$$x_2 = 2020$$
$$x_3 = 505$$
$$x_4 = 504$$
$$x_5 = 126$$
$$x_6 = 125$$
$$x_7 = 124$$
$$x_8 = 31$$
$$x_9 = 30$$
$$x_{10} = 29$$
$$x_{11} = 28$$
$$x_{12} = 7$$
$$x_{13} = 6$$
$$x_{14} = 5$$
$$x_{15} = 4$$
$$x_{16} = 1$$
$$x_{17} = 0$$

16. (B)

By Simon's Favorite Factoring Technique, $ab + a + b + 1 \equiv 1 \pmod{3}$, so $(a+1)(b+1) \equiv 1 \pmod{3}$. Hence, $(a, b) \equiv (0, 0) \pmod{3}$ or $(1, 1) \pmod{3}$. Since $a > b$ "locks" the order, we get $2 \times \binom{33}{2} = 33 \times 32 = 1056$.

17. (C)

Notice that $999 \equiv 0 \pmod{37}$. We also know that $A = 9876543210$ and $B = 123456789$. Since $A \equiv 10 \pmod{37}$ and $B \equiv 36 \pmod{37}$. Thus, $A - B \equiv 10 - 36 \equiv -26 \equiv 11 \pmod{37}$.

18. (E)

In December, there are $31 \equiv 3 \pmod{7}$ days. In November, there are $30 \equiv 2 \pmod{7}$ days. In October, there are $31 \equiv 3 \pmod{7}$ days. In September, there are $30 \equiv 2 \pmod{7}$ days. In August, there are $31 \equiv 3 \pmod{7}$ days. In July, there are $31 \equiv 3 \pmod{7}$ days. In June, there are $30 \equiv 2 \pmod{7}$ days. In May, there are $31 \equiv 3 \pmod{7}$ days. Hence, $3 + 2 + 3 + 2 + 3 + 3 + 2 + 3 \equiv 21 \equiv 0 \pmod{7}$ implies that May 1st in 2021 has the same date as January 1st in 2022.

19. (E)

$$11^{2022} \equiv (11^3)^{674} \pmod{13}$$
$$\equiv (1331)^{674} \pmod{13}$$
$$\equiv 5^{674} \pmod{13}$$
$$\equiv (5^{12})^{56} \cdot 5^2 \pmod{13}$$
$$\equiv 1^{56} \cdot 25 \pmod{13}$$
$$\equiv 12 \pmod{13}$$

20. (B)
Let n be the price of one book. Then, $286n = \overline{5A0B6}$. Since $286 = 2 \times 11 \times 13$, we must make sure that $5 - A + 0 - B + 6 \equiv 0 \pmod{11}$. In other words, $A + B \equiv 0 \pmod{11}$. Hence, $(A, B) = (9, 2), (8, 3), (7, 4), \cdots, (2, 9)$, and $(0, 0)$. Out of 9 pairs of (A, B), we find out that $(A, B) = (6, 5)$ is the only pair such that $\overline{5A0B6}$ is divisible by 13. Hence, $\frac{56056}{286} = 196 = n$. Thus, the sum of digits of n is 16.

21. (C)
From $(0, 0)$ to $(7, 3)$, there are 9 grids that have at least one point of intersection with the line segment. Also, there are 9 additional grids from $(7, 3)$ to $(14, 6)$, so there are 18 grids in total.

22. (D)
Since $496 = 2^4 \cdot 31$, the sum of positive factors equals $(1 + 31)(1 + 2 + 4 + 8 + 16) = 32 \times 31 = 992$. Hence, the sum of digits equals $20 = 9 + 9 + 2$.

23. (D)
First, $P(2021) = 47$. It is obvious that $n > 47$. As we make an observation, we notice that $n = 2 \cdot 48, 2 \cdot 49, 2 \cdot 50$ are the only n-values such that $P(n) > 47$. Hence, there are 3 possible values of n satisfying the given condition.

24. (B)
Let $\overline{ab32}$ be such number. Then, $a + b + 3 + 2 \equiv 0 \pmod 3$ implies that $a + b \equiv 1 \pmod 3$. Thus, we perform caseworks. If $(a, b) \equiv (1, 0) \pmod 3$, then there are 12 possible pairs since $a \in \{1, 4, 7\}$ and $b \in \{0, 3, 6, 9\}$. Likewise, if $(a, b) \equiv (0, 1) \pmod 3$, then there are 9 possible pairs since $a \in \{3, 6, 9\}$ and $b \in \{1, 4, 7\}$. Lastly, if $(a, b) \equiv (2, 2) \pmod 3$, then there are 9 possible pairs since $a, b \in \{2, 5, 8\}$. There are 30 possible pairs of (a, b), which has one-to-one correspondence with the number of four-digit numbers satisfying the given condition.

25. (E)

Let r be the circumradius and k be the length of the other side. Then, $(2r)^2 - k^2 = 900$. Hence,

$$(2r - k)(2r + k) = 900$$
$$2 \cdot 450 = 900$$
$$6 \cdot 150 = 900$$
$$10 \cdot 90 = 900$$
$$18 \cdot 50 = 900$$

There are 13 possible pairs of $(2r - k, 2r + k)$, but pairs with even parities for both coordinates are left out, and $30 \cdot 30 = 900$ is excluded since we are looking at a non-degenerate triangle. Hence, there are 4 possible values of $r = 113, 39, 25$ and 17, if we solve the four cases above.